SADDLEBACK
EDUCATIONAL PUBLISHING

W9-BLZ-979

READING NONFICTION 1

- Biography and Autobiography
- Science and Technology
- History and Geography
- Historic Speeches

READING
in context

PRACTICAL READING 1

PRACTICAL READING 2

READING NONFICTION 1

READING NONFICTION 2

READING FICTION 1

READING FICTION 2

SADDLEBACK
EDUCATIONAL PUBLISHING

Three Watson
Irvine, CA 92618-2767

Website: www.sdlback.com

Development and Production Laurel Associates, Inc.
Cover Design: Elisa Ligon
Interior Illustrations: Ginger Slonaker

ISBN-13: 978-1-56254-191-0
ISBN-10: 1-56254-191-9
eBook: 978-1-60291-320-2

Printed in the United States of America
12 11 10 09 08   9

CONTENTS

A NOTE TO THE STUDENT

Skillful readers have many advantages in life. While they are in school, they obviously get better grades. But the benefits go far beyond the classroom. Good readers are also good thinkers, problem-solvers, and decision-makers. They can avoid many of the problems and frustrations that unskilled readers miss out on. In short, good readers have a much greater chance to be happy and successful in all areas of their lives.

READING IN CONTEXT is an all-around skill-building program. Its purpose is to help you achieve your goals in life by making you a better reader. Each of the six worktexts has been designed with your needs and interests in mind. The reading selections are engaging and informative—some lighthearted and humorous, others quite serious and thought-provoking. The follow-up exercises teach the essential skills and concepts that lead to reading mastery.

We suggest that you thumb through the book before you begin work. Read the table of contents. Notice that each of the four units is based on a unifying theme. Then take a moment to look through the four lessons that make up each theme-based unit. Scan one of the *Before reading* paragraphs that introduces a lesson. Glance at the *Preview* and *Review* pages that begin and end each unit. "Surveying" this book (or any book) in this informal way is called *prereading*. It helps you "get a fix on" the task ahead by showing you how the book is organized. Recognizing patterns is an important thinking skill in itself. And in this case it will make you more comfortable and confident as you begin your work.

Happy reading!

BIOGRAPHY AND AUTOBIOGRAPHY

LESSON 1: The Life and Times of Frederick Douglass

LESSON 2: The Story of My Life (*Helen Keller*)

LESSON 3: Journal of the First Voyage to America
(*Christopher Columbus*)

LESSON 4: Sacajawea

When you complete this unit, you will be able to answer questions like these:

- *Why did African-Americans who had escaped from slavery need to carry "free papers"?*

- *How did Helen Keller first learn the meaning of words?*

- *How did the inhabitants of San Salvador react to the arrival of Columbus?*

- *How did Sacajawea help the Lewis and Clark expedition?*

PRETEST

Write **T** or **F** to show whether you think each statement is *true* or *false*.

1. _____ Attempting to escape from slavery was difficult and dangerous for African-Americans.

2. _____ When Frederick Douglass was caught trying to escape from slavery, he was arrested.

3. _____ People who become blind and deaf at an early age can never learn to read and write.

4. _____ Christopher Columbus gave the natives of San Salvador glass beads in exchange for fresh water.

5. _____ Christopher Columbus visited Japan after sailing away from San Salvador.

6. _____ Sacajawea guided the Lewis and Clark expedition all the way across the western United States to the Pacific coast.

7. _____ For her valuable services to the Lewis and Clark expedition, Sacajawea was paid $10,000.00.

Pretest answers: 1. T 2. F 3. F 4. T 5. F 6. T 7. F

Before reading . . .

An *autobiography* is a person's life story in his or her own words. This lesson presents an adapted excerpt from Frederick Douglass's autobiography. He was the famous African-American abolitionist and writer who became an adviser to President Lincoln. As you read, notice how Douglass reacted to the events along his escape route.

THE LIFE AND TIMES OF FREDERICK DOUGLASS

It was the custom in Maryland to require free black people to have what were called free papers. These identification papers listed the person's name, age, color, and height. Many slaves had escaped by impersonating the owner of one of these sets of papers. A slave who closely resembled the description in the papers would borrow or hire them until he could escape to a free state. Then he would mail the papers back to the owner. This operation was hazardous for the lender as well as for the borrower.

Unfortunately, I did not resemble any of my free acquaintances closely enough. But I had one friend—a sailor—who owned a sailor's protection. This document had a similar purpose to that of free papers. It described the person and certified that he was a free American sailor. I did not match very closely the description on the sailor's protection I borrowed. Close examination of it would have caused my arrest at the start.

In order to avoid this, I decided not to buy a train ticket at the station. Instead, I arranged to have my baggage delivered to the train just as it was starting. I jumped on the car when the train

6

was already in motion. As the train sped on its way, I took a seat in the car for black people. Then the conductor began collecting tickets and examining the papers of his black passengers. My heart was beating anxiously. My whole future depended on the decision of this conductor. When he reached me, he said, "I suppose you have your free papers?" To which I answered, "No, sir; I never carry my free papers to sea with me." Luckily, I had taken the precaution of dressing in a sailor's suit. "But you have something to show that you are a free man, have you not?" "Yes, sir," I answered. "I have a paper with the American eagle on it that will carry me round the world." Then I showed him my sailor's protection. The conductor glanced at it quickly, took my fare, and went on about his business.

Though much relieved, I realized I was still in great danger. Had the conductor looked closer at the paper, it would have been his duty to arrest me. Then I would have been sent back to Baltimore from the first station. After Maryland, I had to pass through Delaware, another slave state. Slave catchers waited at the borders for their prey. Though I was not a murderer fleeing from justice, I felt just as miserable as a criminal. The speeding train seemed to be moving far too slowly.

At Wilmington, I got off the train and took the steamboat for Philadelphia. In making the change I was afraid of being arrested, but no one disturbed me. In Philadelphia, I took the night train for New York, arriving there the next morning. I had completed my journey to freedom in less than 24 hours. This was the end of my experience as a slave.

COMPREHENSION

Write your answers in complete sentences.

1. What people owned free papers, and what was their purpose?

    _____

    _____

2. Why was Douglass unable to use the free papers belonging to
    any of his acquaintances? _____

    _____

3. Why did Douglass decide *not* to buy a train ticket at the station?

    _____

    _____

4. Why was Douglass's heart beating anxiously as the conductor
    approached him? _____

    _____

5. Why did Douglass believe that his whole future depended on
    the decision of the conductor?_____

    _____

6. What kind of identification did Douglass show to the conductor?

    _____

    _____

7. After paying his train fare, why did Douglass believe that he
    was still in great danger? _____

    _____

8. Why did Douglass feel the train was moving too slowly?

    _____

    _____

VOCABULARY

Circle a letter to show the meaning of each **boldface** word. If you need help with meanings, use context clues in the reading.

1. **hazardous**
   a. unpleasant
   b. dangerous
   c. expensive
   d. harmless

2. **baggage**
   a. shipments
   b. containers
   c. compartments
   d. luggage

3. **certified**
   a. asserted
   b. ascertained
   c. confirmed
   d. mentioned

4. **precaution**
   a. safeguard
   b. preparation
   c. prescription
   d. provision

PLOT AND SEQUENCE

Number the events to show which happened first, second, and so on.

_____ Douglass decided not to buy a train ticket at the station.

_____ Douglass got off the train at Wilmington and took the steamboat for Philadelphia.

_____ The conductor asked Douglass for his free papers.

_____ Douglass took the night train from Philadelphia, arriving in New York the next morning.

_____ Douglass jumped on the train after it had already started to move.

_____ Douglass borrowed a sailor's protection from a friend.

_____ Douglass had his baggage delivered to the train just as it was starting.

_____ The conductor began collecting tickets and examining the papers of his black passengers.

DRAWING CONCLUSIONS

Think about the events described in the reading. Based on that information, which of the following statements are reasonable conclusions? Put a checkmark (✔) next to each sensible conclusion.

1. _____ Whenever a free black person allowed someone else to use his or her free papers, there was little chance of either person getting caught.

2. _____ Since Douglass did not resemble his friend very closely, he was taking a big chance by using that man's sailor's protection.

3. _____ Douglass need not have felt so anxious on his journey, because he was not truly in great danger.

4. _____ The sailor's suit Douglass wore probably helped convince the train conductor that the sailor's protection was truly his.

5. _____ Very few African-Americans tried to escape from slavery because most did not wish to be free.

6. _____ When Douglass escaped to freedom, blacks were not allowed to ride in the same train cars as whites.

7. _____ Attempting to escape from slavery took a great deal of courage.

RECALLING IMPORTANT DETAILS

Circle a letter to answer each question.

1. Which of the following appeared on the sailor's protection that Douglass had borrowed?

    a. Douglass's name   c. Douglass's weight and height

    b. Douglass's color   d. an American eagle

2. When the conductor asked Douglass for his free papers, what did Douglass say?

   a. "I left my free papers at home."

   b. "I never carry my free papers to sea with me."

   c. "I loaned my free papers to a friend."

   d. "I lost my free papers and I've applied for new ones."

3. Which of the following was **not** a reason why Douglass felt he was in great danger?

   a. Slave catchers waited at the borders.

   b. He did not match the description of the sailor's protection.

   c. Maryland and Delaware were slave states.

   d. The train from Philadelphia to New York ran only at night.

4. Leaving Wilmington, Douglass took which of the following?

   a. the steamboat for New York

   b. the train for New York

   c. the train for Philadelphia

   d. the steamboat for Philadelphia

PUZZLER

One or more words in each sentence is written backward. Find these words, circle them, and write them correctly on the lines below. The first one is done for you.

1. Many slaves escaped by (gnitanosrepmi) the owner of a set of free papers.   _impersonating_

2. I did not elbmeser closely enough any of my free secnatniauqca.

   _____

3. I degnarra to have my egaggab delivered to the train as it was starting.

   _____

4. Though I was not a reredrum, I felt just as elbaresim as a lanimirc.

   _____

Before reading . . .

At the age of 19 months, a girl named Helen Keller was stricken with a devastating illness. It severely affected her speech and left her blind and deaf. This lesson presents an adapted excerpt from her autobiography. As you read, notice how Helen reacts to things most of us take for granted.

THE STORY OF MY LIFE

I was six the morning my teacher came in 1886. She led me into her room and gave me a doll. When I had played with it a little while, Miss Sullivan slowly spelled into my hand the word "d-o-l-l." I was at once interested in this finger play and tried to imitate it. When I finally succeeded in making the letters correctly, I was flushed with childish pleasure and pride. Running downstairs to my mother, I held up my hand and made the letters for the word *doll*. I did not know that I was spelling a word—or even that words existed. I was simply making my fingers go in monkey-like imitation. In the days that followed I learned to spell a great many words in this uncomprehending way. It was several weeks later before I understood that everything has a name.

One day, I was playing with my new doll. Then Miss Sullivan put my big rag doll into my lap. She also spelled "d-o-l-l" and tried to make me understand that "d-o-l-l" applied to both the object and the word. Earlier in the day we had had a tussle over the words "m-u-g" and "w-a-t-e-r." Miss Sullivan had tried to impress upon me that "m-u-g" is *mug* and "w-a-t-e-r" is *water*—but I persisted in confounding the two. In despair, she had dropped the subject for the time, only to renew it at the first opportunity. I soon became impatient at her repeated attempts. Seizing the new doll, I dashed it upon the floor. I was keenly delighted when I felt the fragments of the broken doll at my feet. Neither sorrow nor regret followed my passionate outburst. I had not loved the doll. In the still, dark world in which I lived there was no strong sentiment or tenderness. I felt my teacher sweep the fragments to one side of the hearth. I had a sense of satisfaction that the cause of my discomfort was removed. When she brought me my hat, I knew I was going out into the warm sunshine. This thought—if a wordless sensation may be called a thought—made me hop and skip with pleasure.

We walked down the path to the well-house. I was attracted by the fragrance of the honeysuckle there. Someone was drawing water, and my teacher placed my hand under the spout. As the cool stream gushed over one hand, she spelled the word *water* into the other. First she spelled the word slowly, then rapidly. I stood still, my whole attention fixed upon the motions of her fingers. Suddenly, I felt a misty consciousness as of something forgotten—a thrill of returning thought. It was then that the mystery of language was somehow revealed to me. I knew that "w-a-t-e-r" meant the wonderful cool something that was flowing over my hand! That living word awakened my soul—gave it light, hope, joy, set it free! There were barriers still, it is true, but barriers that could in time be swept away.

W

COMPREHENSION

Write **T** if the statement is *true* or **F** if the statement is *false*. Write **NI** for *no information* if the article does not provide that information.

1. _____ Right from the start, Helen knew that everything had a name.

2. _____ Spelling the word "d-o-l-l" with her fingers filled Helen with pride.

3. _____ The first time Helen made the letters "d-o-l-l," she knew it was a word, and she knew what the word meant.

4. _____ Helen's parents were pleased at her progress in learning how to make letters with her hands.

5. _____ Helen and Miss Sullivan had gotten into a tussle because Helen kept confusing *mug* with *water*.

6. _____ Helen's parents hired Miss Sullivan because she had experience working with severely disabled people.

7. _____ Helen removed the source of her discomfort by throwing her new doll on the floor.

8. _____ Water flowing over one hand while the letters "w-a-t-e-r" were spelled out into her other hand taught Helen what a word was.

SENTENCE COMPLETION

Choose eight words from the box to complete the sentences below.

sensation	consciousness	sentiment	passionate
flushed	uncomprehending	barriers	fragrance
tussle	confounding	opportunity	imitation

1. Helen learned to spell a great many words in an

   _____ way.

2. Helen and Miss Sullivan had had a _____

   over the words "m-u-g" and "w-a-t-e-r."

3. Neither sorrow nor regret followed Helen's _____

   outburst.

4. There was no strong _____ in the dark

   world in which Helen lived.

5. Both Helen and Miss Sullivan were attracted by the

   _____ of the honeysuckle.

6. Suddenly, Helen felt a misty _____, as of

   something forgotten.

7. Helen was _____ with childish pleasure and

   pride when she succeeded in making the letters correctly.

8. At first, Helen made her fingers go in monkey-like

   _____.

IDENTIFYING PARTS OF SPEECH

Nouns are words that name a person, place, or thing. *Verbs* tell about an action or state of being. Read the following words from the article. Write **N** if the word is a *noun*, or **V** if the word is a *verb*.

____ tussle	____ living	____ running	____ fragrance
____ spelled	____ pride	____ teacher	____ doll
____ playing	____ imitate	____ applied	____ opportunity
____ dashed	____ hearth	____ attention	____ honeysuckle
____ removed	____ attracted	____ barriers	____ swept
____ fragments	____ sunshine	____ called	____ gushed

DRAWING CONCLUSIONS

Put a checkmark (✔) next to the best answer to each of the following questions.

1. Helen learned to spell many words once she learned how to make letters with her hands. What conclusion can you draw from this fact?

   a. _____ Although Helen was severely disabled, she was very intelligent and a quick learner.

   b. _____ At first, Helen didn't understand what words were, and she was not much interested in learning.

   c. _____ Helen was just pretending to not understand what words were.

   d. _____ Helen found that learning to spell was a boring activity.

2. In a passionate outburst, Helen broke her new doll. What conclusion can you draw from this fact?

   a. _____ Helen did not get along very well with Miss Sullivan.

   b. _____ Helen resented having to learn anything new.

   c. _____ Helen was impatient with Miss Sullivan's teaching. Believing her new doll was the source of the problem, Helen threw it to the floor.

   d. _____ Helen was frustrated. She wanted Miss Sullivan to give up trying to teach her anything.

3. Helen had a sudden insight about the connection between the water flowing on her hand and the word *water*. Should this be considered a major turning point in her life?

   a. _____ No. Just because she made this one connection did not mean she would continue to make such connections.

   b. _____ No. Making just one connection was not such a big deal.

   c. _____ Yes. Understanding one word meant that from now on there was nothing she couldn't learn.

   d. _____ Yes. Now she would always understand the meaning of *water*.

PUZZLER

Fill in each blank with the word from the reading that answers the question. Then unscramble the circled letters to learn the name of a system of writing for the blind. The first one has been done for you.

1. What did Miss Sullivan give to Helen at their first meeting?

D O (L) L

2. What did Helen learn to "write" with her fingers?

(_) _ _ _ _ _ _

3. What did Helen feel when she first succeeded in making letters correctly?

_ _ (_) _ _

4. After several weeks, Helen learned that everything has a what?

_ (_) _ _

5. What happened between Helen and Miss Sullivan over the words "m-u-g" and "w-a-t-e-r"?

_ _ _ _ _ (_)

6. As the cool stream gushed over Helen's hand, what word did Miss Sullivan spell?

_ _ _ _ (_)

7. What did Helen believe would be swept away in time?

(_) _ _ _ _ _ _ _

The name of a system of writing for the blind:

_ _ _ _ _ _ _

Before reading . . .

A *journal,* or *diary,* is a person's daily account of events and personal reactions. This lesson presents an adapted excerpt from Christopher Columbus's journal. How does the famous explorer react to the new world he is seeing for the first time? His account begins nine days after landing on the island of San Salvador.

JOURNAL OF THE FIRST VOYAGE TO AMERICA

Sunday, October 21, 1492. At 10 o'clock, we arrived at a cape of the island [San Salvador]. We anchored there, the other vessels also. After having eaten a meal, I went ashore with my crew to view the country.

This island even exceeds the others in beauty and fertility. Groves of lofty trees are everywhere. Large lakes are surrounded by the overhanging trees. Everything looks as green as Andalusia [Spain] in April. The melody of the birds was so exquisite that one felt unwilling to part from the spot. The sky was filled with flocks of parrots. They were very different in appearance from those of our country. We came across a thousand different sorts of trees. Their fruits gave off a wonderful and delicious aroma. It was a great sadness to me that I knew nothing about them. I am certain they are all valuable, so I have collected some samples and preserved them.

Going around one of these lakes, I saw a snake. Upon being discovered, he took to the water. We followed him, as the water was not deep. When we caught up with him, we killed him with our lances. I have kept the skin for Your Highnesses [King Ferdinand and Queen Isabella of Spain].

I think there are many more such snakes around here. I also discovered an aloe tree, which I am told is valuable. Tomorrow, I am determined to take a portion of it onboard the ship.

While we were in search of good water, we came upon a village of the natives. The inhabitants fled in fear, carrying off their goods to the mountain. I ordered that nothing they had left behind should be taken. Soon we saw several of the natives coming toward our party. One of them came up to us. We gave him some glass beads, with which he was delighted. In return, we asked him for water. After I had gone aboard the ship, the natives came down to the shore with their calabashes full of water. They showed great pleasure in presenting us with the water. I ordered that more glass beads be given them. They promised to return the next day.

It is my wish to fill all the water casks of the ships at this place. Then I shall depart immediately. If the weather permits, I shall sail around the island. I hope to succeed in meeting with the king. I hear that he has gold— and I want to see if I can acquire any of it. Afterwards, I shall set sail for another very large island which I believe to be Cipango [Japan]. If I find gold or spices in abundance there—or on any of the other islands—I shall decide what to do. At all events, I am determined to proceed on to the continent. My plan is to visit the city of Guisay [Kublai Khan's City of Heaven]. There I shall deliver the letters of Your Highnesses to the Great Khan. Then I shall demand an answer, with which I shall return.

COMPREHENSION

Write your answers in complete sentences on the lines.

1. Why did Columbus and his crew go ashore on the island of San Salvador? _____

   _____

2. Why did the fruits on the trees make Columbus feel sad?

   _____

3. What did Columbus hear that pleased him so much? _____

   _____

4. What did Columbus intend to do with the skin of the snake he and his crew had killed? _____

   _____

5. What did the natives of San Salvador do when they saw Columbus and his crew approaching their village? _____

   _____

6. What sort of trade took place between Columbus and the natives of the village? _____

   _____

7. Why was Columbus interested in meeting the king of the island?

   _____

8. What did Columbus intend to do when he met with the Great Khan?

   _____

   _____

VOCABULARY

Circle a letter to show the meaning of the **boldface** word from the reading.
If you're not sure, use context clues to help you decide.

1. **cask**
   a. barrel
   b. casket
   c. case
   d. cast

2. **exquisite**
   a. exceptional
   b. extreme
   c. beautiful
   d. extensive

3. **calabash**
   a. cabbage
   b. caliper
   c. cauldron
   d. gourd

4. **fertility**
   a. versatility
   b. capability of producing fruit
   c. festivity
   d. diversity

5. **abundance**
   a. absoluteness
   b. plentifulness
   c. thoroughness
   d. completeness

FACT OR OPINION?

Read the following statements about Columbus's journal. Write **F** if the statement is a *fact*, and **O** if the statement is an *opinion*.

1. _____ Columbus arrived at a cape of the island of San Salvador on Sunday, October 21, 1492.

2. _____ San Salvador was the most beautiful and fertile of all the islands.

3. _____ Anybody who heard the melody of the birds on San Salvador would want to stay there forever.

4. _____ The fruits were certainly very valuable.

5. _____ Columbus and his crew killed the snake with their lances.

6. _____ There must be many such snakes around the lakes.

7. _____ Trading glass beads for water was a fair exchange.

8. _____ The king of the island had huge quantities of gold.

9. _____ Gold and spices were surely to be found on the island of Cipango.

10. _____ Columbus was carrying letters from King Ferdinand and Queen Isabella to present to the Great Khan.

PUZZLER

Fill in the blanks with words from the journal that answer the questions. Then unscramble the circled letters to learn what name Columbus gave to the natives of San Salvador. The first one has been done for you.

1. What color did Columbus notice on the island?   G R E E (N)

2. Who was the Queen of Spain?   (_) _ _ _ _ _ _ _

3. What did Columbus use to kill the snake?   _ _ (_) _ _

4. What did Columbus need to get from the natives?   _ (_) _ _ _

5. What did Columbus collect and preserve?   _ _ _ (_) _ _

6. What kinds of birds filled the sky?   _ _ _ _ _ _ (_)

7. Who was the King of Spain?   _ _ _ (_) _ _ _ _

The name Columbus gave to the natives:

_ _ _ _ _ _ _

DRAWING CONCLUSIONS

Think about the information recorded in Columbus's journal. Then decide which of the following statements are reasonable conclusions. Put a checkmark (✔) next to each sensible conclusion.

1. _____ Columbus had a keen appreciation for the beauty of nature.

2. _____ Columbus had little regard for King Ferdinand and Queen Isabella.

3. _____ Previously, Columbus had seen parrots in Spain.

4. _____ The natives of the village were afraid that Columbus and his crew would steal their possessions.

5. _____ The natives of the village did not lack fresh water.

6. _____ One of the goals of Columbus's voyage was to acquire gold and spices.

7. _____ It doesn't take long to sail from San Salvador to Japan.

8. _____ King Ferdinand and Queen Isabella were very interested in hearing from the Great Khan.

RECALLING DETAILS

The following items contain details from the journal entry. Put a checkmark (✔) in front of the correct answer.

1. What kind of tree did Columbus want to take away a part of?

____ palm   ____ aloe

____ pine   ____ oak

2. What was the Great Khan's name?

____ Ferdinand   ____ Guisay

____ Kublai   ____ His Highness

3. What was Columbus's name for Japan?

____ Salvador   ____ Guisay

____ Andalusia   ____ Cipango

4. What was the name of the City of Heaven?

____ Guisay   ____ Andalusia

____ Cipango   ____ Salvador

Before reading . . .

A *biography* is a form of nonfiction in which a writer tells the life story of another person. The following article is a brief biography of the famous Native American, Sacajawea. She was the famous Native American who guided the Lewis and Clark expedition through the western United States in the early 1800s. As you read, notice how the writer has included opinion along with the factual information.

SACAJAWEA

Sacajawea was a Shoshone Indian whose name meant "Bird Woman." She was born in what is now Idaho, sometime between 1786 and 1789. When she was still a little girl, her village was raided. Minnetaree warriors kidnapped her and took her to their village. She was enslaved for several years. Then a French-Canadian fur trader named Toussaint Charbonneau came to visit the Minnetaree. He gambled with the Minnetaree and ended up a winner. His prize was the Indian girl Sacajawea.

Charbonneau took Sacajawea away with him. They went to the land of the Mandan Indians— in what is now North Dakota. There he made Sacajawea his wife. In fact, however, she was little more than a slave. She was put to work making clothes and harvesting the beans, corn, and squash grown by the Mandans.

In November 1804, an expedition of white men arrived in the country of the Mandans. President Thomas Jefferson had sent them. They were exploring the vast new Louisiana Territory, which the United States had just purchased from France. The 40-member group was led by Captain Meriwether Lewis and

Lieutenant William Clark. They had started out in St. Louis and traveled up the Missouri River. They spent the winter among the friendly Mandans.

Lewis and Clark's mission was to first find the source of the Missouri River. Then they were to cross the Rocky Mountains and go all the way to the Pacific Ocean. After meeting Charbonneau and Sacajawea, Lewis and Clark were impressed. They persuaded the couple to serve as their guide and interpreter. In the spring, the expedition set out across the plains. Sacajawea carried her infant son Pomp on her back. She was excited about the possibility of returning to the land of the Shoshone.

By August, they had reached the Rocky Mountains. There they met a band of Shoshone. While Sacajawea was interpreting for Lewis and Clark, she recognized a Shoshone as her brother, Cameauhwait. She began to leap up and down and yell joyfully. Cameauhwait, who was a chief, agreed to help the expedition by providing horses. The rest of the trip was very difficult. They traveled through snowy weather along icy mountain trails. Sacajawea still carried Pomp on her back. On October 16, 1805, they reached the Columbia River. But because of its many rapids and whirlpools, they had to carry their boats much of the time. Finally, on November 17, they reached the Pacific Ocean. They spent the winter on the beach.

The expedition returned to Mandan country in August 1806. Sacajawea, Pomp, and Charbonneau left the expedition there. Charbonneau was paid $500.00 for his help. Without Sacajawea, the expedition might have ended in failure. But she received nothing for her valuable services. She is believed to have died in 1812.

COMPREHENSION

Write your answers in complete sentences on the lines.

1. Why do you think the exact dates of Sacajawea's birth and death are not known? _____

2. Why did President Thomas Jefferson send out an expedition in 1804? _____

   _____

3. Why did Lewis and Clark need the services of a guide and an interpreter? _____

   _____

   _____

4. Why did Lewis and Clark choose Charbonneau and Sacajawea to serve as guide and interpreter? _____

   _____

   _____

5. Why did Sacajawea get excited after the expedition met the band of Shoshone? _____

   _____

6. What obstacles did the expedition face on the journey across the mountains and down the Columbia River? _____

   _____

   _____

SENTENCE COMPLETION

Choose six words from the box to complete the sentences below.

expedition	**mission**	**guide**	**interpreter**
whirlpools	**enslaved**	**gambled**	**recognized**

1. Sacajawea _____ one of the Shoshone as her brother.

2. Charbonneau _____ with the Minnetaree.

3. Lewis and Clark's _____ was to find the source of the Missouri River, cross the Rocky Mountains, and go all the way to the Pacific Ocean.

4. An _____ can translate one language into another.

5. Sacajawea was kidnapped and _____ by the Minnetaree.

6. In November 1804, an _____ of white men arrived in the country of the Mandans.

RECALLING DETAILS

Circle a letter to correctly answer each question.

1. Sacajawea belonged to which of the following tribes?

   a. Mandan   b. Minnetaree   c. Shoshone   d. Cherokee

2. Which of the following tasks did Lewis and Clark **not** have to accomplish?

   a. find the source of the Missouri River

   b. cross the Rocky Mountains

   c. explore the deserts of the Southwest

   d. go all the way to the Pacific Ocean

3. Which of the following vegetables did Sacajawea **not** have to harvest in Mandan country?

    a. beans   b. squash   c. potatoes   d. corn

4. In which of the following states was Sacajawea born?

    a. North Dakota   b. Oregon   c. Washington   d. Idaho

5. Which river was so wild that the expedition members had to carry their boats much of the time?

    a. Missouri River   c. Columbia River

    b. Mississippi River   d. Colorado River

6. On which date did the expedition reach the Pacific Ocean?

    a. November 17, 1804   c. November 17, 1805

    b. October 16, 1805   d. August 17, 1806

FACT OR OPINION?

Think about the information given in the reading. Then read the following statements. Write **F** if the statement is a *fact* or **O** if the statement is an *opinion*.

1. _____ Sacajawea was a Shoshone Indian whose name meant "Bird Woman."

2. _____ Sacajawea would have had an easier life had she remained with the Shoshone.

3. _____ Charbonneau was very happy with the prize he won by gambling with the Minnetaree.

4. _____ Charbonneau and Sacajawea lived in Mandan country.

5. _____ Although she was Charbonneau's wife, Sacajawea was little more than a slave.

28

6. _____ Without Sacajawea, the expedition might have ended in failure.

7. _____ Considering Sacajawea's valuable service to the expedition, Lewis and Clark did not treat her fairly.

PUZZLER

Use information from the reading to help you complete the crossword puzzle. The puzzle words are answers to the questions.

ACROSS

2. From which country did the United States purchase the Louisiana Territory?

5. The main task of the Lewis and Clark expedition was to do what?

6. What kind of goods did Charbonneau trade?

7. Which ocean did the expedition reach?

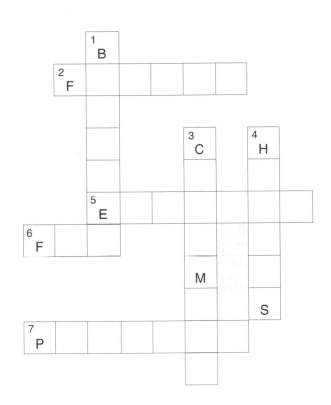

DOWN

1. How was Cameauhwait related to Sacajawea?

3. Which river had many wild rapids and whirlpools?

4. What did Cameauhwait provide for the expedition?

— REVIEW —

FACTS ABOUT AUTOBIOGRAPHIES AND BIOGRAPHIES

Write **T** if the statement is *true* or **F** if the statement is *false*.

1. _____ A biography is a form of nonfiction in which a writer tells the life story of another person.

2. _____ An autobiography is a form of fiction in which a person tells his or her own life story.

3. _____ A journal is a daily autobiographical account of events and personal reactions.

4. _____ *The Life and Times of Frederick Douglass* is a biography.

5. _____ *The Story of My Life* is an autobiography by Helen Keller.

6. _____ *Journal of the First Voyage to America* is a biographical account of Columbus's voyage of exploration.

7. _____ *Sacajawea* is a brief biography of the Shoshone woman who served as guide and interpreter for the Lewis and Clark expedition.

8. _____ If you were to write the story of your own life, you would be writing a biography.

9. _____ If your best friend were to write the story of your life, he or she would be writing a biography.

10. _____ If you kept a daily account of the events in your life, you would be keeping a journal or diary.

11. _____ An autobiography can only be written by a very old person.

12. _____ A biography can only be written about a famous person.

Unit 2

SCIENCE AND TECHNOLOGY

LESSON 1: The World's Largest Cat

LESSON 2: The Red Planet

LESSON 3: Fuel Cells: Cheaper, Cleaner Power

LESSON 4: Hurricanes: Killer Storms

When you complete this unit, you will be able to answer questions like these:

■ *On what continent do Siberian tigers live?*

■ *Why is Mars referred to as the "red planet"?*

■ *How will fuel cells change the way we get energy?*

■ *How do hurricanes form?*

PRETEST

Write **T** or **F** to show whether you think each statement is *true* or *false*.

1. _____ Those who have studied tigers and lions say that the lion is more powerful.

2. _____ The Siberian tiger is the world's largest cat.

3. _____ Mars is the fourth planet from the sun.

4. _____ Although Mars is like Earth in many ways, it would be a cold, harsh place for humans.

5. _____ The ruins of ancient cities have been discovered on Mars.

6. _____ Fuel cells generate electricity through a chemical reaction that creates little or no air pollution.

7. _____ Because they are so expensive, fuel cells will never be a practical source of energy.

8. _____ Hurricanes are powerful storms, and it's lucky that they seldom strike the United States.

Pretest answers: 1. F 2. T 3. T 4. T 5. F 6. T 7. F 8. F

Before reading . . .

How big is *big*? A very large housecat may weigh nearly 30 pounds. But even the heaviest tomcat wouldn't stand much of a chance against its relative, the Siberian tiger. The largest Siberian tiger on record weighed almost 850 pounds! Read on to learn more about this amazing animal.

THE WORLD'S LARGEST CAT

Just how big is the Siberian tiger? An average adult male is about 12 feet long and weighs some 650 pounds. Measured at the shoulder, its height is about 42 inches. There is great power in the tiger's heavily muscled yet graceful body. Its only rival in strength and fierceness is the lion. Yet those who have studied both cats say the tiger is more powerful.

The Siberian tiger lives in Asia. It can be found in northern China and Korea as well as in the northernmost part of Russia called Siberia. Its cold homeland is covered in snow for much of the year. That's why the huge tiger's constant search for food involves many long journeys. The Siberian's range is much larger than that of any other kind of tiger.

Hunting is a full-time job for the Siberian tiger. Only about one in ten of its hunting trips is successful. Like all tigers, the Siberian is a carnivore, or meat-eater. It preys mainly on deer and wild pigs, but it also eats fish. This is how the Siberian stalks its prey: First, it creeps to within 30 to 80 feet of its victim. Then it pounces and grabs the prey by the nape of the neck. Small prey is instantly killed by the neck bite. But larger prey is brought to the ground and killed with a suffocating bite to the throat.

WILL THEY DISAPPEAR?

At one time there were eight different kinds of tigers in existence. Today, three of these are extinct, and the remaining five are on the endangered list. It is estimated that there are no more than 200 Siberian tigers left in the wild. That means that there are nearly as many Siberian tigers in captivity as there are roaming free.

What happens if the tiger misses its prey on the pounce? It may give chase for 600 feet or so, but it rarely catches the would-be victim. After a kill, the tiger drags its prey to cover. When it has eaten its fill, it covers up the remains and goes to sleep. Later it eats the rest of the carcass.

Like all tigers, the Siberian wears a distinctive coat of stripes. But the Siberian tiger's coat is a lighter color than that of its much smaller cousin, the Bengal tiger. Its topcoat is a yellowish white under its dark stripes. Its undersides are white, extending to the back legs and tail. During the harsh winters, the Siberian's coat grows even paler. This adaptation helps it blend in with its snowy environment.

Nature has adapted this magnificent tiger in other ways as well. Low temperatures in the Siberian's habitat may fall to 50 degrees below zero. For this reason, it grows a longer, thicker coat than other tigers. And for even more insulation, it also develops an extra layer of fat on its flanks and belly.

COMPREHENSION

Write **T** if the statement is **true** or **F** if the statement is **false**. Write **NI** for **no information** if the article does not provide that information.

1. _____ The female Siberian tiger is about half the size of the male.

2. _____ Experts on big cats think the tiger is more powerful than the lion.

3. _____ A Siberian tiger eats its kill at the same place it brings it down.

4. _____ Only a few Siberian tigers live in India.

5. _____ The Siberian tiger is just over four feet tall.

6. _____ The coat of a Bengal tiger is darker than that of a
Siberian tiger.

7. _____ Blind at birth, newborn Siberian tiger cubs don't open
their eyes for about two weeks.

PUZZLER

First, unscramble the words from the article.

ERPY	**SINGOATCUFF**	**HATBAIT**
_____	_____	_____
PEAN	**MONTRENVINE**	**TIXCENT**
_____	_____	_____
RETILT	**SCENERIFES**	**DEPADAT**
_____	_____	_____

Then use the unscrambled words to complete the sentences.

1. An endangered species may one day be _____.

2. Wild pigs and deer are the main _____ of the
Siberian tiger.

3. Nature has _____ the Siberian to survive in
very cold weather.

4. A tiger grabs its prey by the _____ of the neck.

5. There are usually three or four cubs in a tiger's _____.

6. The lion is the Siberian's only rival in strength and

_____.

7. Northern Asia is the Siberian tiger's _____.

8. The _____ of the Siberian tiger is cold and snowy.

9. Large prey is killed with a _____ bite to the throat.

ANTONYMS

Draw a line to match each word from the article with its *antonym* (word that means the opposite) on the right. Then write sentences using the **boldface** words.

1. **solitary**   a. plant-eater

2. **extinct**   b. flees

3. **distinctive**   c. social

4. **capitivity**   d. commonplace

5. **carnivore**   e. freedom

6. **stalks**   f. existent

7. _____

8. _____

9. _____

10. _____

11. _____

12. _____

SYNONYMS

Synonyms are words that have the same or nearly the same meaning.
In each group of words, circle the synonym of the **boldface** word.

1. **rival**   relative   competitor   team   predator

2. **flanks**   legs   backbone   sides   cheeks

3. **habitat**   homeland   den   adaptation   climate

DRAWING CONCLUSIONS

What reasonable conclusion can be drawn from each statement?
Circle a letter to show the logical conclusion.

1. Adult females usually live in family units.

   a. Male tigers protect the cubs.
   b. Females teach the cubs to hunt.
   c. Female tigers are very fearful.

2. The Siberian tiger's range is larger than that of any other kind of tiger.

   a. Siberians live much longer.
   b. Siberians are restless animals.
   c. The Bengal's habitat has more food.

3. The Siberian creeps up on its prey before pouncing.

   a. Tigers hunt much as house cats do.
   b. Lions are better hunters than tigers.
   c. The prey can hear the tiger coming.

SUFFIXES

Decide which *suffix* (word ending) should be added to each **boldface** word in
parentheses. Then write the new word to complete each sentence. Hint: You
will *not* use all the suffixes, and some will be used more than once.

-n	-ed	-ity	-ly	-ful	-t	-d	-ing	-ion	-ed	-ied	-s

1. There is great power in the tiger's (**heavy**) _____

   (**muscle**) _____ yet (**grace**) _____ body.

2. Those who have (**study**) _____ both the lion and the tiger say the tiger is more (**power**) _____.

3. The (**Siberia**) _____ tiger lives (**main**) _____ on deer and wild pigs.

4. Small prey is (**instant**) _____ (**kill**) _____ by a bite on the nape of the neck.

5. For more (**insulate**) _____ from (**freeze**) _____ temperatures, the Siberian develops an extra layer of fat.

6. There are about 200 Siberian (**tiger**) _____ in (**captive**) _____.

COMPOUND WORDS

A *compound word* is made up of two or more parts. Using word parts from the box, complete each sentence with the correct compound word.

in	land	sides	under
span	life	home	with

1. A Siberian tiger's _____ are white, extending to the back legs and tail.

2. Its cold _____ is covered in snow for much of the year.

3. Before it pounces, the tiger creeps to _____ 30 to 80 feet of its prey.

4. The Siberian tiger's _____ is about 20 years.

Before reading . . .

Much of what we know about the planet Mars is scientific fact. But people have also had their *opinions* about Mars. For example, many have debated whether or not life exists there. Watch out for the difference between fact and opinion. As you read this article, notice when the writer is stating a fact and when the writer is expressing an opinion.

THE RED PLANET

Mars, the fourth planet from the sun, is often called the "red planet" because of its reddish-orange color. It is one of the most beautiful planets in the solar system. The unusual color is caused by chemicals in the soil. Because of its fiery color, the Romans named the planet after their god of war. The Greeks called it Ares, in honor of their own god of battle. While Earth has one moon, Mars has two—Phobos and Deimos, named for two of the sons of Ares and Aphrodite. In Greek, *Phobos* means *fear*, and *Deimos* means *terror*. Either the Greeks had a vivid imagination or perhaps they had some reason to be afraid of the moons of Mars!

Mars is about 141 million miles from the sun. The distance between Mars and Earth varies. It can range from about 47 million miles to about 233 million miles—when the two planets are on opposite sides of the sun. Mars is about half the size of Earth, and it takes twice as long to orbit the sun. It is the most Earthlike planet in the solar system. Both planets have seasons, and both have an atmosphere—although the Martian atmosphere is very thin. The Martian day is about the same length as a day on Earth. Mars is the only planet besides Earth where liquid water is known to have flowed across the surface. And like Earth, Mars has polar ice caps. These can be seen through a telescope.

Scientists have learned much about Mars by observing it through telescopes. But the most detailed information has come from space probes. In 1960, the Soviets launched the first space probe to Mars. In the 1960s and 1970s, the United States launched the *Mariner* and *Viking* probes. For many years, some people believed that intelligent life existed on Mars. Astronomers had detected patterns of straight lines on the red planet. They thought these were canals built by the Martians. Then the *Viking 1* space probe landed a robot explorer on the surface of Mars. The *Viking* lander tested samples of Martian soil—but found no samples of life. The *Pathfinder* probe, launched by NASA in 1996, also found no signs of life.

The various space probes have sent back photographic images of the planet's surface. The scenery resembles a barren desert landscape in Arizona. Mars also has canyons, long valleys, and giant volcanoes. One of them, Olympus Mons, is 16 miles high. It is the largest volcano in the solar system. Although Mars is like Earth in many ways, it would be a cold, harsh place for humans. The temperature on the surface ranges from a low of about −225° F to a high of about 65° F. The air there is too thin to breathe. Huge dust storms sometimes cover the whole planet. Yet, sometime in the 21st century, humans will walk on Mars. Perhaps they will discover that life still exists somewhere on Mars—or that it existed there in the past.

COMPREHENSION

Write your answers in complete sentences on the lines.

1. What causes the reddish color of Mars? _____

    _____

2. Why did the Romans name the planet *Mars*? _____

    _____

3. From what source have we gotten most of our detailed information

    about Mars? _____

    _____

4. What did the *Viking* lander discover when it tested samples of

    the Martian soil? _____

    _____

5. Why would Mars be a harsh place for humans? _____

    _____

6. When are Earth and Mars the greatest distance apart? _____

    _____

RECALLING DETAILS

Circle a letter to answer each question.

1. Which of the following is **not** a way in which Earth and Mars
   are similar?

    a. Both planets have
       atmospheres.

    b. Both planets have
       seasons.

    c. Both planets have
       breathable atmospheres.

    d. Both planets have
       polar ice caps.

2. Which of the following was **not** a Greek name?

   a. Deimos   b. Mars   c. Ares   d. Phobos

3. What is the distance from Mars to the sun?

   a. 47 million miles   c. 141 million miles

   b. 233 million miles   d. 225 million miles

4. What is the *greatest* distance between Earth and Mars?

   a. 225 million miles   c. 233 million miles

   b. 47 million miles   d. 141 million miles

5. Which of the following is a true statement?

   a. Olympus Mons is 6 miles high.   c. Olympus Mons is the second tallest volcano on Mars.

   b. Olympus Mons is 10 miles high.   d. Olympus Mons is taller than any volcano on Earth.

6. What is the temperature *range* on the surface of Mars?

   a. 225° F   b. 65° F   c. 85° F   d. 290° F

FACT OR OPINION?

Read the following statements from the article. Write **F** if the statement is a *fact* or **O** if the statement is an *opinion*.

1. _____ It is one of the most beautiful planets in the solar system because of its reddish color.

2. _____ Because of its fiery color, the Romans named the planet after their god of war.

3. _____ Either the Greeks had a vivid imagination, or perhaps they had some reason to be afraid of the moons of Mars.

4. _____ The Martian day is about the same length as a day on Earth.

5. _____ In 1960, the Soviets launched the first space probe to Mars.

6. _____ The scenery on Mars resembles a barren desert in Arizona.

7. _____ Astronomers thought they saw canals built by the Martians.

8. _____ Scientists have learned much about Mars by observing the planet through telescopes.

9. _____ The air on Mars is too thin for humans to breathe.

10. _____ Sometime in the 21st century, humans will walk on Mars.

SENTENCE COMPLETION

Choose six words from the box to complete the sentences below.

orbit	surface	chemicals	volcano
canals	probe	atmosphere	telescopes

1. The reddish color of Mars is caused by _____ in the soil.

2. The *Viking 1* space _____ landed a robot explorer on Mars.

3. The Martian _____ is very thin.

4. Olympus Mons is the largest _____ in the solar system.

5. Liquid water is known to have flowed across the _____.

6. Mars takes twice as long as Earth to _____ the sun.

PUZZLER

Use the clues to help you complete the crossword puzzle.

ACROSS

3. layer of air surrounding a planet

5. Martian moon whose name means "fear"

7. NASA Martian space probe launched in 1996

9. They launched the first space probe to Mars in 1960.

DOWN

1. Much of Martian surface consists of this.

2. Greek name for Mars

4. a planet's path around the sun

6. No signs of this have yet been found on Mars.

8. Martian moon whose name means "terror"

IDENTIFYING PARTS OF SPEECH

Nouns are used to name a person, place, or thing. *Verbs* are used to describe an action or state of being. Read the **boldface** words from the article. Then write **N** if the word is a *noun* or **V** if the word is a *verb*.

____ chemicals	____ planets	____ caused	____ atmosphere
____ liquid	____ flowed	____ learned	____ information
____ launched	____ believed	____ life	____ tested
____ humans	____ landed	____ volcano	____ temperature
____ breathe	____ scenery	____ canals	____ discover

Before reading . . .

Imagine a world without air pollution. Such a world is in fact just around the corner. This is thanks to the development of the fuel cell—a cheaper, cleaner, and more efficient type of energy technology. As you read this article, notice when the writer is stating facts about fuel cells and when the writer is expressing opinions.

FUEL CELLS: CHEAPER, CLEANER POWER

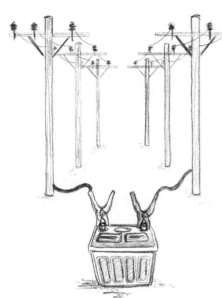

The electric utility business in the United States is old-fashioned. It still relies on the same delivery system it has used for a hundred years. That may be about to change. A house in Albany, New York, proves this point. Since 1998, it has been running on electricity from a fuel cell device about the size of a refrigerator. Fuel cells generate electricity. They do this through a chemical reaction that emits little or no air pollution. The device works by combining oxygen and an energy source such as hydrogen. The hydrogen molecules in the fuel cell are broken up into protons and electrons. The protons then pass through a membrane, which is a type of filter. After that, they mix with the oxygen to produce water vapor. The electrons cannot pass through the membrane. Electricity is created when they are forced to go around it. This process, of course, avoids the use of pollution-causing fossil fuels such as oil or coal. That's why it is amazingly clean.

In addition to providing a cleaner source of power, fuel cells offer two other important advantages. They provide a backup supply of electricity, and a source of power for homes located far away from current electric lines.

Sometimes utilities cannot keep up with our increasing demand for electricity. The result is often a power brownout—a partial cutback in electric service. Some areas have even experienced blackouts—a total cutoff of electricity. In a blackout, anyone without electric power during a heat wave is out of luck. No electricity means no air conditioning. And anyone without power during a severe cold spell is left to freeze in the dark. Fuel cells would eliminate a reduction or loss of electric power.

Fuel cells have actually been around for some time. For decades, NASA has been using fuel cells for electricity and water on space missions. But only now are fuel cells being developed for the American consumer. It is clear that fuel cells are a practical source of energy for homes or businesses. But fuel cells are also being developed to power automobiles, trucks, and buses. Vehicles powered by fuel cells will be totally nonpolluting. Ford Motor Company Chairman Bill Ford, Jr. recently said, "I believe fuel cells will finally end the 100-year reign of the internal combustion engine." All the major automobile manufacturers seem to agree. They have promised to have fuel-cell vehicles available within the next three to five years.

What will happen as fuel cells begin to replace existing energy technologies? The world will breathe a lot easier. Cleaner air means healthier lungs. No pollution particles, like soot, means no more burning eyes or throats due to smog. The use of fuel cells for electricity in rural areas will make a big difference, too. Our countryside will no longer be cluttered by miles of ugly power lines! As amazing as it may seem, a world without air pollution is truly just around the corner.

COMPREHENSION

Write **T** if the statement is *true* or **F** if the statement is *false*. Write **NI** for *no information* if the article does not provide that information.

1. _____ Today's electric utility business uses a very different delivery system than the one used a hundred years ago.

2. _____ Fuel cells deliver electricity through a chemical reaction that gives off little or no air pollution.

3. _____ Protons in a fuel cell pass through a membrane, but electrons do not.

4. _____ People who live in California are more interested in fuel cells than those who live in New York.

5. _____ For the last five years, the city of Detroit has been testing a fleet of buses powered by fuel cells.

6. _____ There has never been a time when electric utilities could not meet increased demands for electric power.

7. _____ People who lose their electric power during a heat wave are unable to use their air conditioners.

8. _____ All the major automobile manufacturers are developing fuel-cell vehicles.

RECALLING DETAILS

Circle a letter to answer each question.

1. Which of the following is **not** an advantage of fuel cells?

   a. cleaner source of power

   b. backup supply of electricity

   c. free electric power

   d. source of power for homes too far from current electric lines

2. Fuel cells generate electricity through a chemical reaction that combines which two elements?

   a. hydrogen and water vapor

   b. oxygen and water vapor

   c. hydrogen and oxygen

   d. water vapor and air

3. The fuel cell process provides a clean source of power because it avoids which of the following?

   a. use of fossil fuels

   b. use of electricity

   c. use of hydrogen

   d. use of oxygen

4. Which of the following did **not** happen whenever utilities failed to keep up with increased demand for electricity?

   a. power brownout

   b. power blackout

   c. reduction of electric power

   d. no change in electric power

5. For which of the following means of transportation are fuel cells **not** being developed?

   a. buses   b. airplanes   c. automobiles   d. trucks

SYNONYMS

Synonyms are words that have the same or nearly the same meaning.
In each group of words, circle the synonym of the **boldface** word.

1. **relies**   relates   realizes   depends   replies

2. **generate**   promote   produce   endanger   enervate

3. **membrane**   brain   member   embrace   filter

4. **eliminate**   remove   replace   repair   relinquish

5. **molecule**   monocle   monocyte   particle   partition

FACT OR OPINION?

Read the following statements. Write **F** if the statement is a *fact* or **O** if the statement is an *opinion*.

1. _____ New technologies are always better than old ones.

2. _____ Fuel cells generate electricity through a chemical reaction.

3. _____ Electric power lines stretching across the countryside are an ugly sight.

4. _____ Fuel cells do not use pollution-causing fossil fuels.

5. _____ Every person in the world will be better off when fuel cells replace the current means of producing electricity.

6. _____ NASA has been using fuel cells on space missions for several decades.

7. _____ Some areas of the country occasionally experience power brownouts or blackouts.

8. _____ People may not want to buy fuel cell automobiles if they are more expensive than other cars.

9. _____ Fuel cells will replace the internal combustion engine within the next few years.

10. _____ The way the electric utility business generates and sells electric power may be about to change.

PUZZLER

In each sentence, two or more words are spelled backward. Find these words, circle them, and write them correctly on the lines below. The first one is done for you.

1. Fuel cells (etareneg) electricity through a (lacimehc) reaction.
   _____generate_____   _____chemical_____

2. The snotorp pass through a enarbmem, a type of retlif.
   _____

48

3. Vehicles derewop by fuel cells will be totally gnitullopnon.

   _____

4. Fuel cells would elanimile a reduction or loss of cirtcele power.

   _____

5. Fuel-cell selcihev will be elbaliava within the next three to five years.

   _____

SENTENCE COMPLETION

Choose six words from the box to complete the sentences below.

generate	**membrane**	**combustion**	**pollution**
brownouts	**vehicles**	**molecules**	**blackouts**

1. Some areas of the country experienced _____, a total cutoff of electricity.

2. Fuel cells may finally replace the internal _____ engine.

3. Fuel cells _____ electricity through a chemical reaction.

4. All the major automobile manufacturers are developing fuel-cell _____.

5. The hydrogen _____ in the fuel cell are broken up into protons and electrons.

6. The protons pass through a _____, a type of filter.

Before reading . . .

You know that hurricanes can cause tremendous destruction. That's why scientists are trying to learn more about these killer storms. More knowledge can reduce the danger to lives and property. As you read this article, notice the important numerical data included.

HURRICANES: KILLER STORMS

Every year, one or more hurricanes hit the East or Gulf Coasts of the United States. Every so often, one of these storms will cause a huge amount of damage. Fortunately, scientists have learned how to track these killer storms. To do this, they use data from radar and weather satellites. They also get information from planes that fly into the hurricanes. The National Hurricane Center in Florida issues warnings to those in the path of an approaching hurricane. Before the storm strikes, residents of coastal and other low-lying areas are evacuated. Thanks to hurricane warnings, many lives are saved. But there is little that can be done to prevent massive property damage.

Just how destructive are hurricanes? A glance at statistics from recent years tells the story. In 1972, Hurricane Agnes caused $3 billion in damage and 134 deaths. In 1989, Hurricane Hugo caused $4 billion in damage and more than 50 deaths. And in 1992, Hurricane Andrew set a record. It caused more than $20 billion in estimated damages and killed 60 people. Some two million people were evacuated from their homes. Andrew was the most expensive natural disaster in U.S. history.

How do such monstrous storms form? Typically, a hurricane is born when warm air moves west over the Sahara Desert in Africa. Suppose this warm air mass then moves over warm seawater in the eastern part of the Atlantic Ocean. When that happens, a tropical disturbance develops. If conditions are right, the disturbance will develop into a hurricane. When ocean water evaporates, it releases additional heat into the atmosphere. This adds energy to the developing storm. The system then intensifies even more. It gets worse when winds near the ocean's surface combine with the disturbance. The combination causes the winds to spiral inward. Soon the system begins to spin like a pinwheel, and its forward motion adds speed to the winds.

At the center, or the "eye," of the hurricane, the winds are calm and the air pressure is very low. The eye averages about 15 miles in diameter. Surrounding the eye is the eyewall—the area of strongest winds and heaviest rains. Heat and water vapor from the ocean's surface rush upward through the eyewall. Eventually, wind and water spill across the top of the system.

Hurricane winds can extend outward about 150 miles from the eye. Gale-force winds can reach out as far as 300 miles. Hurricane intensity is measured according to the speed of its winds—on a scale of 1 to 5. A Category 1 hurricane has winds of from 74 to 95 m.p.h. (miles per hour). Hurricane Andrew was a Category 4. It had wind gusts of over 175 m.p.h. The strongest, Category 5, is rare. It has sustained winds of over 155 m.p.h. A hurricane usually travels at speeds ranging from about 5 to 20 m.p.h. But unusually powerful hurricanes have been known to move as fast as 50 m.p.h.

COMPREHENSION

Write **T** if the statement is *true* or **F** is the statement is *false*. Write **NI** for *no information* if the article does not provide that information.

1. _____ Every year, at least one hurricane hits the United States.

2. _____ Scientists still have no way to track a hurricane.

3. _____ Hurricanes sometimes strike the coastal region of New England.

4. _____ The National Hurricane Center issues warnings to people who live in the path of an approaching hurricane.

5. _____ Hurricane Agnes caused more damage than Hurricane Hugo.

6. _____ Hurricane Andrew was the most expensive natural disaster in U.S. history.

7. _____ Hurricanes develop from tropical disturbances over the eastern part of the Atlantic Ocean.

8. _____ When ocean water evaporates, heat is released into the atmosphere.

9. _____ The strongest winds are in the eye of the hurricane.

10. _____ Hurricanes lose their force as soon as they hit land.

UNDERSTANDING NUMERICAL DATA

Scientific facts are often supported by numerical data. The following items contain numerical details from the article about hurricanes. Circle a letter to show the correct answer to each question. Look back at the article if you need help.

1. Hurricane Agnes caused which of the following?

   a. $4 billion in damage and more than 50 deaths

   c. $4 billion in damage and 60 deaths

   b. $3 billion in damage and 134 deaths

   d. more than $20 billion in damage and 134 deaths

2. Hurricane Hugo struck the United States in which year?

    a. 1972   b. 1989   c. 1990   d. 1992

3. Hurricane Andrew caused which of the following?

    a. $3 billion in damage and 134 deaths

    b. $4 billion in damage and more than 50 deaths

    c. more than $20 billion in damage and 60 deaths

    d. $3 billion in damage and 60 deaths

4. What is the average diameter of the eye of a hurricane?

    a. 15 miles   b. 50 miles   c. 150 miles   d. 300 miles

5. How far can hurricane winds extend outward from the eye?

    a. 50 miles   b. 100 miles   c. 150 miles   d. 300 miles

6. What is the strength of sustained winds in a Category 5 hurricane?

    a. over 74 miles per hour

    b. over 125 miles per hour

    c. over 155 miles per hour

    d. over 175 miles per hour

7. At what speed does a hurricane usually travel?

    a. 5 to 20 miles per hour

    b. 20 to 35 miles per hour

    c. 35 to 50 miles per hour

    d. over 50 miles per hour

DRAWING CONCLUSIONS

Think about the information in the article. Then put a checkmark (✔) next to each reasonable conclusion.

1. _____ People living along the East and Gulf Coasts of the United States are more likely to be affected by hurricanes than those living farther inland.

2. _____ The National Hurricane Center in Florida is a useless organization because it is unable to prevent damage to property.

3. _____ If a hurricane is approaching, the best thing to do is to lock the door and windows and hide under the bed.

4. _____ Many lives are saved when people in the path of an approaching hurricane are evacuated from their homes.

5. _____ Scientists now have a pretty good idea of how hurricanes form.

6. _____ A tropical disturbance will only develop into a hurricane if the conditions are right.

7. _____ Andrew, a Category 4 hurricane, would have caused even more damage if it had been a Category 5 hurricane.

8. _____ The strongest Category 5 hurricane would not cause much damage if it did not strike a populated area.

9. _____ Because a car can easily outrun a hurricane, it is not necessary to leave home until the hurricane is only a few miles away.

VOCABULARY

Circle a letter to show the meaning of the **boldface** word.

1. **sustained**
   a. variable
   b. gusty
   c. constant
   d. suspended

2. **evacuated**
   a. supported
   b. assisted
   c. removed
   d. evicted

3. **intensity**
   a. strength
   b. direction
   c. damage
   d. effects

4. **statistics**
   a. weather reports
   b. written record
   c. history
   d. numerical data

PUZZLER

Fill in the blanks with words from the article that answer the questions. Then unscramble the circled letters to learn what a hurricane in the Pacific Ocean is called. The first one has been done for you.

1. What part of a hurricane surrounds the eye?

   E (Y) E W A L L

2. What kind of winds are indicated by a hurricane's category number?

   _ _ _ (_) _ _ _ _ _

3. What was the name of the 1989 hurricane that caused more than 50 deaths?

   (_) _ _ _

4. Hurricanes can cause massive damage to what?

   _ _ _ (_) _ _ _ _

5. What was the name of the 1992 hurricane that caused more than $20 billion in damages?

   _ (_) _ _ _ _

6. What kind of disturbance will develop into a hurricane if the conditions are right?

   _ _ (_) _ _ _ _ _

7. Water from what source releases heat into the atmosphere when it evaporates?

   (_) _ _ _ _ _

The name of a hurricane in the Pacific Ocean:

_ _ _ _ _ _ _

—— REVIEW ——

RECALLING SCIENTIFIC DETAILS

Circle a letter to correctly answer each question.

1. How big is the Siberian tiger?

   a. 8 feet long, 450 pounds

   b. 10 feet long, 550 pounds

   c. 12 feet long, 650 pounds

   d. 14 feet long, 850 pounds

2. What causes the reddish color of Mars?

   a. dust in the Martian atmosphere

   b. chemicals in the air of Mars

   c. chemicals in the Martian soil

   d. clouds in the Martian sky

3. Why would Mars be a difficult place for humans to live?

   a. very high mountains and polar ice

   b. thin air and very cold temperatures

   c. very cold temperatures and vast deserts

   d. deep canyons and cold temperatures

4. Fuel cells generate electricity through a chemical reaction that combines which two elements?

   a. hydrogen and water vapor

   b. oxygen and water vapor

   c. hydrogen and oxygen

   d. water vapor and air

5. How strong are the winds in the eye of a hurricane?

   a. the winds are calm

   b. 50–75 miles per hour

   c. 75–125 miles per hour

   d. 125–155 miles per hour

HISTORY AND GEOGRAPHY

LESSON 1: First Glimpse of the Sierra *(John Muir)*

LESSON 2: The Final Battle of the War of 1812

LESSON 3: The Travels of Marco Polo

LESSON 4: The Mystery of Machu Picchu

When you complete this unit, you will be able to answer questions like these:

■ *Why did John Muir call the Sierras "the Range of Light"?*

■ *Why should the Battle of New Orleans* not *have been fought?*

■ *What did Marco Polo write about in his travel book?*

■ *What was the real "lost city" of the Incas?*

PRETEST

Write **T** or **F** to show whether you think each statement is *true* or *false*.

1. _____ John Muir liked to hike in the mountains, but he preferred to spend time in big cities.

2. _____ The mountain range known as the Sierras is located in California.

3. _____ The United States sent Andrew Jackson and his army to attack the British in New Orleans.

4. _____ The British wanted to negotiate an end to the War of 1812 because they were losing to the Americans.

5. _____ Marco Polo described the city of Ormus as an important center of trade and commerce.

6. _____ Machu Picchu was built by the ancient Incas in the Andes Mountains of Peru.

7. _____ Although often referred to as one of the wonders of the world, Machu Picchu is seldom visited by tourists.

Pretest answers: 1.F 2.T 3.F 4.F 5.T 6.T 7.F

Before reading . . .

In 1868, the Scots immigrant John Muir settled in California. He would spend much of the rest of his life hiking up and down the Sierras, exploring natural wonders such as Yosemite Valley. This lesson presents an adapted excerpt from Muir's journal. It describes his first impressions of California and the Sierras. Notice when he is stating facts and when he is expressing opinions.

FIRST GLIMPSE OF THE SIERRA

Arriving by the Panama steamer, I stopped one day in San Francisco. I immediately inquired for the nearest way out of town. "But where do you want to go?" asked the man to whom I had applied for this important information. "To any place that is wild," I said. This reply startled him. He seemed to fear that I might be crazy. From his point of view, the sooner I was out of town the better. He promptly directed me to the Oakland ferry.

So on the 1st of April, 1868, I set out afoot for Yosemite. It was the bloom-time of the year over the lowlands and coastal ranges. The landscapes of the Santa Clara Valley were fairly drenched with sunshine. All the air was quivering with the songs of the meadowlarks. The hills were so covered with flowers that they seemed to be painted. Slow, indeed, was my progress through these glorious gardens— the first of the California flora I had seen. Cattle and cultivation were making few scars as yet. I wandered enchanted in long, wavering curves. By my pocket map I knew that Yosemite Valley lay to the east, and that I should surely find it.

One shining morning, I looked eastward from the summit of Pacheco Pass. The landscape displayed before me, after all my wanderings, still appears as the most beautiful I have ever beheld! At my feet lay the Great Central Valley of California. It was level and flowery, like a lake of pure sunshine. The valley appeared to be 40 or 50 miles wide and about 500 miles long. It was one rich, furred garden of yellow composite.

From the eastern boundary of this vast golden flowerbed rose the mighty Sierra. It was miles in height, and so gloriously colored— so radiant—it seemed not clothed with light, but wholly composed of it like the wall of some celestial city. Along the top and extending a good way down was a rich pearl-gray belt of snow. Below that was a belt of blue and dark purple, marking the extension of the forests. Stretching along the base of the range was a broad belt of rose-purple. All of these colors, from the blue sky to the yellow valley, smoothly blended as they do in a rainbow. The effect was a wall of light ineffably fine.

It seemed to me that the Sierra should be called by another name. Not the Nevada or Snowy Range—but the Range of Light. For 10 years I have been wandering and wondering in the heart of it. I have never stopped rejoicing in its glorious floods of light—from the white beams of the morning streaming through the passes to its noonday radiance on the crystal rocks. As I think now of the flush of the alpenglow, and the irised spray of countless waterfalls, it still seems, above all others, the Range of Light.

COMPREHENSION

Write your answers in complete sentences on the lines.

1. When Muir reached California, what was he most interested in doing?

   _____

2. How did Muir plan to travel to the Sierra?

   _____

3. Why was Muir so sure that he would find Yosemite Valley?

   _____

4. What landscape did Muir consider the most beautiful he had
   ever seen? _____

   _____

5. Why did Muir compare the mountains of the Sierra range to the
   walls of a celestial city? _____

   _____

6. What did Muir think the Sierra ought to be called? _____

   _____

FACT OR OPINION?

Think about the information in the reading. Then read the statements below.
Write **F** if the statement is a *fact* or **O** if the statement is an *opinion*.

1. _____ Muir arrived in San Francisco aboard the Panama steamer.

2. _____ Muir set out for Yosemite on the 1st of April, 1868.

3. _____ The view looking eastward from Pacheco Pass is the most
   beautiful sight in the world.

4. _____ The hills were so covered with flowers that they seemed to be painted.

5. _____ The Great Central Valley of California is 500 miles long.

6. _____ The mighty Sierra appeared radiant and gloriously colored.

7. _____ Along the top of the mountains and extending downward was a band of snow.

8. _____ The mountains seemed to be composed of light.

9. _____ The Sierra ought to be called the Range of Light.

IDENTIFYING PARTS OF SPEECH

Adjectives describe a person, place, or thing. Read the following words from the article. Put a checkmark (✔) in front of each adjective.

___ important	___ landscapes	___ sunshine	___ beautiful
___ mighty	___ rainbow	___ countless	___ golden
___ yellow	___ broad	___ noonday	___ flowery
___ level	___ rich	___ celestial	___ appears
___ summit	___ glorious	___ wandering	___ spray

DRAWING CONCLUSIONS

Put a checkmark (✔) next to each reasonable conclusion that can be drawn from information in the article.

1. _____ Muir was more interested in spending time in the wilderness than in a city.

2. _____ Muir always avoided traveling by train.

61

3. _____ The weather in the Great Central Valley of California was sunny all year long.

4. _____ Muir had a deep appreciation for the beauty of nature.

5. _____ Muir had quite an imagination—no landscape could possibly be as colorful as Muir's description of the Sierra.

6. _____ Muir would have preferred that the Santa Clara Valley always remain free of cattle and cultivation.

7. _____ After hiking through the Sierra for 10 years, Muir still had the same impression of that mountain range.

PUZZLER

Fill in the blanks with the words from the article that answer the questions. Then unscramble the circled letters to learn the feature for which Yosemite is famous. The first one has been done for you.

1. How did Muir travel in California?   W A (L) K I N G

2. What was Muir's first stop in California?   _ (_) _   _ (_) _ _ _ (_) _ _

3. What kind of area in California did Muir want to explore?   (_) _ (_) _ _ _ _ (_) _ _

4. What valley was still relatively free of cattle and cultivation?   _ _ _ (_) _   _ _ _ _ (_)

5. What made the hills of the Santa Clara Valley seem like they were painted?   (_) _ _ _ _ _ _ _

The natural feature for which Yosemite is famous:

_ _ _ _ _ _ _ _ _ _ _ _

VOCABULARY

Circle a letter to show the meaning of each **boldface** word. Check a dictionary if you need help.

1. **drenched**
   a. quenched
   b. soaked
   c. squirted
   d. sprayed

2. **quivering**
   a. trembling
   b. trickling
   c. questioning
   d. quarelling

3. **ineffably**
   a. inefficiently
   b. indescribably
   c. indirectly
   d. intuitively

4. **enchanted**
   a. engulfed
   b. entangled
   c. distracted
   d. charmed

5. **radiant**
   a. radical
   b. bright
   c. radioactive
   d. happy

6. **celestial**
   a. cellular
   b. celebratory
   c. heavenly
   d. spectacular

7. **cultivation**
   a. distributing books
   b. raising crops
   c. exhibiting works of art
   d. studying philosophy

8. **alpenglow**
   a. aurora
   b. alpenstock
   c. alpenhorn
   d. reddish glow

RECALLING DETAILS

Put a checkmark (✔) in front of the detail that correctly answers each question.

1. How did Muir travel from San Francisco to Oakland?

   ___ train   ___ stagecoach   ___ walking   ___ ferry

2. In what direction did Muir travel to get to the Sierra?

   ___ north   ___ east   ___ south   ___ west

3. Where did Muir get his first glimpse of the Sierra?

   ___ San Francisco   ___ Pacheco Pass

   ___ Santa Clara Valley   ___ Great Central Valley

4. How wide did Muir estimate the Central Valley to be?

   ___ 500 miles   ___ 100 miles   ___ 40–50 miles   ___ 10 miles

Before reading . . .

Only 29 years had passed since the United States had defeated Britain in the Revolutionary War. Now the two nations were entering into a second war against each other. The reading in this lesson is about the closing days of the War of 1812. As you read, notice how important dates are when you draw conclusions about historical events.

Andrew Jackson at the
Battle of New Orleans

THE FINAL BATTLE
OF THE WAR OF 1812

By December 24, 1814, the United States and Great Britain had been fighting each other for more than two years. On that day, American and British negotiators signed a peace treaty at Ghent, Belgium. The peace negotiations had begun in August of that year. At that time, both nations had begun to grow weary of the war. Henry Clay and John Quincy Adams were members of the American team of negotiators.

The peace treaty made no mention of the causes of the war. Both countries had agreed that the serious issues that had led to the war would all be resolved at a later date. These issues had to do with free trade, the rights of seamen, and disputes over boundary lines. As far as the negotiators were concerned, the war was over with the signing of the treaty. All combatants could now lay down their arms. But was the war really over? Unfortunately, in 1814, there were no telephones or telegraphs. Word traveled slowly. People in America—British as well as American— did not know that a peace treaty had been signed.

While peace negotiations were going on, the British had ordered an attack on New Orleans. They hoped to win a decisive victory. Their success would put pressure on the Americans to agree to peace terms favorable to the British. General Andrew Jackson learned of the British plans at the last minute. His soldiers had given him the nickname "Old Hickory." Why? Because it was the toughest substance they could think of. Jackson made hasty preparations to defend New Orleans. He commanded an army of troops from Kentucky, Tennessee, and Louisiana. Joining them were free African-American volunteers and Choctaw Indians, as well as the pirate Jean Lafitte and his men.

On the morning of January 8, 1815—a full 15 days after the signing of the Treaty of Ghent—the British launched their attack. They began by shooting a rocket into the air. Marching in front of his 6,000 troops, General Packenham led the British assault. Jackson's men were greatly outnumbered. They waited in their trenches until the British came within firing range. Then the Americans let loose. One round of artillery and rifle fire followed another. The British soldiers went down, row after row—cut to pieces by the American guns! Before long, more than 2,000 British soldiers had been either killed or wounded. Among the dead were General Packenham and two other British generals. The Battle of New Orleans, the bloodiest of the war, was over— and the Americans had won! Amazingly, there were only 21 American casualties.

News of the American victory reached Washington, D.C., on February 11. Word arrived that same day of the signing of the Treaty of Ghent! President James Madison was given credit for defending the honor of the United States. At last the war was truly over. Now relations could improve between America and Britain. The two nations would never again go to war with each other.

COMPREHENSION

Write your answers in complete sentences.

1. Why did the Americans and British meet at Ghent to try to negotiate a peace treaty? _____

   _____

2. Why wasn't the war over as soon as the Treaty of Ghent was signed? _____

   _____

3. Why did the British order an attack on New Orleans? _____

   _____

4. Why had General Andrew Jackson been given the nickname "Old Hickory"? _____

   _____

5. Why did Jackson have to make hasty preparations to defend New Orleans? _____

   _____

6. What effect did the end of the War of 1812 have on relations between the United States and Great Britain? _____

   _____

RECALLING DETAILS

Circle a letter to answer each question below.

1. Which of the following was **not** an issue that led to the War of 1812?

   a. free trade

   b. boundary disputes

   c. religious freedom

   d. the rights of seamen

66

2. When did America and Britain begin peace negotiations at Ghent?

   a. December 1814   c. August 1814

   b. January 1815   d. February 1815

3. Which of the following states did **not** contribute soldiers to Jackson's army?

   a. Kentucky   c. Tennessee

   b. Louisiana   d. Pennsylvania

4. How many days after the signing of the Treaty of Ghent did the British launch their attack on New Orleans?

   a. 7 days   b. 15 days   c. 30 days   d. 42 days

5. When did word of the signing of the Treaty of Ghent reach Washington, D.C.?

   a. December 24, 1814   c. January 8, 1815

   b. January 2, 1815   d. February 11, 1815

SENTENCE COMPLETION

Choose eight words from the box to complete the sentences below.

artillery	disputes	negotiators	launched	outnumbered
casualties	resolved	combatants	decisive	preparations

1. Amazingly, there were only 21 American _____.

2. The serious issues that led to the war would be _____ later.

3. American and British _____ _____ signed a peace treaty at Ghent.

4. The British hoped to win a _____ victory at New Orleans.

5. Once the treaty was signed, all _____ could lay down their arms.

6. Jackson made hasty _____ to defend New Orleans.

7. The Americans let loose one round of _____ and rifle fire after another.

8. Jackson's men were greatly _____ by the British forces.

PUZZLER

One or more words in each sentence has been spelled backward. Find these words, circle them, and write them correctly on the lines below. The first one is done for you.

1. Peace (snoitaitogen) began in August 1814.

   negotiations

2. Unfortunately, in 1814, there were no senohpelet or shpargelet.

   _____

3. The British began their attack by gnitoohs a tekcor into the air.

   _____

4. More than 2,000 British soldiers had either been dellik or dednuow.

   _____

SEQUENCE OF EVENTS

Number the events to show which happened first, second, and so on.

_____ Andrew Jackson prepares to defend New Orleans.

_____ News of the American victory reaches Washington, D.C., just as word arrives of the signing of the Treaty of Ghent.

_____ The British order an attack on New Orleans.

_____ American and British peace negotiators sign the Treaty of Ghent.

_____ The American troops at New Orleans begin firing on the British troops.

_____ America and Britain decide to hold peace negotiations at Ghent.

_____ The Americans win a decisive victory at the Battle of New Orleans.

_____ The British troops begin their attack by shooting a rocket into the air.

DRAWING CONCLUSIONS

Put a checkmark (✔) next to each reasonable conclusion that can be drawn from information in the article.

1. _____ The British were not serious when they entered into peace negotiations with the Americans.

2. _____ The Battle of New Orleans should never have been fought.

3. _____ The Americans won the Battle of New Orleans because General Jackson's military strategy was superior to General Packenham's.

4. _____ Although America and Britain signed a peace treaty, the issues leading to war were too serious to be resolved.

Before reading . . .

In the year 1295, Marco Polo, a trader from Venice, Italy, returned home. For many years he had been traveling throughout Asia. Most of the distant lands he had explored had never before been visited by a European. Along the way, Polo carefully described all of the places, people, and customs he encountered. His writings were based on his own observations as well as information given to him by others. As you read, decide which statements seem to be based on fact and which do not.

THE TRAVELS OF MARCO POLO

In the Indian Ocean—upon an island not far from the mainland—stands a city named Ormus. Its port is visited by traders from all parts of India. They bring spices, precious stones, pearls, gold, elephant's teeth, and various other articles of merchandise. Other traders purchase these items, which are then spread throughout the world. Ormus is the main commercial city in the kingdom of Kierman. But there are other towns and castles in the kingdom. They are on the Plain of Ormus, on the mainland. Rukmedin Achomak is the ruler of Ormus. He is, in turn, ruled by the King of Kierman. Whenever a foreign merchant dies in Ormus, Achomak confiscates his property and deposits it in his treasury.

The inhabitants of Ormus are dark-colored Muslims. They sow their wheat, rice, and other grain in November and reap their harvest in March. They gather dates in May. The food of the natives is different from ours. Were they to eat wheat bread and red meat, their health would suffer. They live mainly on dates and salted fish.

During the summer season, the people of Ormus do not remain in the city. The extreme heat makes the air unhealthy. Instead, the citizens stay at their gardens. They are located along the shore on the mainland or on the banks of the river. In these summer retreats, they construct huts over the water. They enclose one side with stakes driven into the land below the water. On the other side they make a covering of leaves to shelter them from the sun. All summer long, a daily land-wind blows from about nine o'clock until noon. This wind is so intensely hot that it makes breathing difficult. People exposed to it can even die by suffocating. On the sandy Plain of Ormus, none who are overtaken by the wind can escape from its effects. As soon as the people notice the approach of this wind, they immerse themselves in water up to their chins. They stay in the water until the wind stops blowing.

One year, the ruler of Ormus neglected to pay his tribute to the King of Kierman. So the King sent an army to collect it by force. Since it was summer, the people of Ormus were on the mainland. The King sent 1,600 soldiers on horseback and 500 on foot to surprise them. Unfortunately, the army was misled by their guides. They failed to reach their intended destination before nightfall. They had to stop in a grove not far from Ormus. As they began traveling the next morning, they were assailed by the hot wind. So *they* were the ones who were surprised! The entire army suffocated. Not even a single soldier escaped to carry the terrible news back to the King. When the people of Ormus learned of the event, they came to bury the bodies. The dead soldiers had been badly baked by the intense heat. When they were moved, their limbs separated from the rest of their bodies. It was necessary to dig the graves close to the spot where the bodies lay.

COMPREHENSION

Write **T** if the statement is *true* or **F** if the statement is *false*. Write **NI** for *no information* if the article does not provide that information.

1. _____ The city of Ormus stood on an island in the Indian Ocean, not far from the mainland.

2. _____ Ormus was an important center of trade and commerce.

3. _____ The inhabitants of Ormus ate mainly dates and salted fish.

4. _____ Dozens of new boats were built each year at Ormus.

5. _____ The ruler of Ormus was also the ruler of the kingdom of Kierman.

6. _____ During the intense summer heat, the people of Ormus did not remain in the city.

7. _____ Every day in the summer, the wind brought some relief from the heat.

8. _____ The huts built by the people of Ormus were six feet above the surface of the water.

SENTENCE COMPLETION

Choose 10 words from the box to complete the sentences below.

merchandise	reap	confiscates	commercial
inhabitants	tribute	immerse	enclosed
destination	sow	assailed	exposed

1. When a foreign merchant dies, Achomak _____ his property.

2. Ormus is the main _____ city in the kingdom of Kierman.

3. The soldiers failed to reach their intended _____
   before nightfall.

4. The people _____ themselves in water when
   the hot wind begins to blow.

5. One year the ruler of Ormus neglected to pay his
   _____ to the King of Kierman.

6. People _____ to the winds of Ormus can
   die by suffocating.

7. There were many kinds of _____ for sale in Ormus.

8. As the soldiers began traveling the next morning, they were
   _____ by the hot wind.

9. One side of the hut was _____ with stakes
   driven into the land under the water.

10. The people _____ their wheat, rice, and other
    grain in November.

FACT OR FICTION?

Some of the following statements reflect factual things that Marco Polo may
have seen with his own eyes. Other statements seem more like fiction. They
probably reflect stories that were told to Marco Polo. Write **FA** if the statement
is a *fact* or **FI** if the statement is *fictitious*.

1. _____ The inhabitants of Ormus were Muslims.

2. _____ The ruler of Ormus was named Rukmedin Achomak.

3. _____ An entire army of 2,100 soldiers died of suffocation from
   the hot wind.

4. _____ The people of Ormus gathered dates in May.

5. _____ The soldiers had been so badly baked that their limbs separated from their bodies.

RECALLING DETAILS

Circle a letter to answer each question.

1. Where is the city of Ormus located?

   a. near the Plain of Ormus

   b. in the middle of the mainland

   c. by the banks of a river

   d. on an island in the Indian Ocean

2. Which of the following did the people of Ormus sow in November?

   a. wheat, dates, and other fruit

   b. rice, fruit, and other grain

   c. wheat, rice, and other grain

   d. wheat, rice, and dates

3. The people of Ormus ate mainly which of the following?

   a. wheat bread and red meat

   b. salted fish and wheat bread

   c. dates and rice

   d. dates and salted fish

4. In summer, the people of Ormus avoid which of the following?

   a. the city of Ormus

   b. banks of the river

   c. huts over the water

   d. gardens along the shore

5. The army sent by the King of Kierman consisted of which of the following?

   a. 500 soldiers on horseback and 1,600 on foot

   b. 300 soldiers on foot and 500 on horseback

   c. 600 soldiers on foot and 400 on horseback

   d. 1,600 soldiers on horseback and 500 on foot

PUZZLER

Use the clues to help you complete the crossword puzzle.

ACROSS

2. name of city ruled by Achomak

5. Achomak's people leave the city during this season.

6. type of stones bought and sold on an island in Indian Ocean

7. articles offered for sale or purchase

8. what happened to the King of Kierman's soldiers

DOWN

1. what Achomak had to pay each year to the King of Kierman

3. where Achomak deposited the confiscated property

4. Achomak's first name

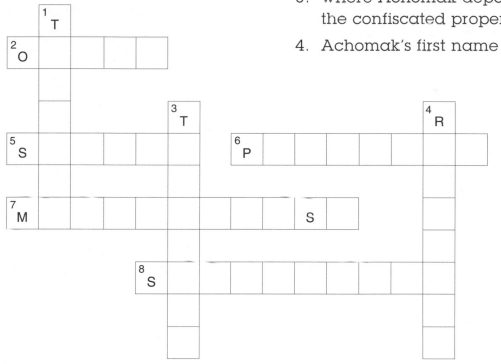

ANTONYMS

Antonyms are words that have opposite meanings. In each group, circle the antonym of the **boldface** word.

1. **gather**   attract   collect   distribute   contribute

2. **purchase**   buy   sell   trade   barter

3. **precious**   expensive   valuable   worthless   dear

4. **terrible**   wonderful   awful   dreadful   horrible

Before reading . . .

High up in the Andes Mountains of Peru is the ancient Incan city of Machu Picchu. Archeologists have learned much about the Incas through studying these ruins. But there are still unsolved mysteries. As you read this article, try to notice the differences between facts and opinions.

THE MYSTERY OF MACHU PICCHU

Machu Picchu is often referred to as one of the wonders of the world. The ruins of this city in the Andes are truly an amazing sight. At an elevation of 7,710 feet, it sits on a saddle between two sharp mountain peaks. Just below, llamas walk along terraced slopes. Farther below—2,000 feet straight down—is the rushing Urubamba River. In the distance are snow-covered mountains that rise as high as 20,000 feet.

Machu Picchu is believed to have been built by the Incas in about the year A.D. 1400. In 1532, the Spaniards arrived in South America and promptly destroyed the Incan civilization. But because Machu Picchu was situated in such an inaccessible location, the Spaniards never found it. For the next few centuries, Machu Picchu was forgotten. Then, in 1911, an American archeologist named Hiram Bingham discovered Machu Picchu. He had been searching for Vilcabamba, the lost city of the Incas. At first, he thought the ruin he had stumbled upon *was* Vilcabamba. The real Vilcabamba, however, was discovered elsewhere in the Andes by American archeologists in 1961.

Every year, thousands of visitors from all over the world visit Machu Picchu. They marvel at the spectacular ruins so high up on a steep mountain. They wonder how the Incas carried the huge stones for the buildings up the mountain. We only know that the Incas were great builders and were able to do amazing things. They knew how to farm steep mountain slopes by cutting terraces. They grew more than 60 types of plants and developed 250 kinds of potatoes. To bring water to their fields, they built stone aqueducts. Their long, fine roads kept their empire connected. They built stone temples and houses, and they made retaining walls to hold soil in place. The huge stones that they cut fit together perfectly. Their stone buildings still stand in many places—even though earthquakes are common in the Andes Mountains.

The descendents of these ancient people still live in the Andes. They speak the old language of the Incas, known as *Quechua*. Just as the Incas used to do, some of them use a knotted string called a *quipu* to keep track of their animal herds.

Machu Picchu's original purpose is shrouded in mystery. There are houses, temples, palaces, and courtyards. There are water and irrigation systems, fountains, and observation towers. There are walkways and thousands of steps—consisting of stone blocks as well as footholds carved into the rock. These walkways connect the plazas, residential areas, terraces, the cemetery, and the major buildings. There is also a huge stone sundial. The ancient Incas are known to have worshipped the sun god. Was Machu Picchu used mainly as a religious ceremonial center? Was it truly a city? Perhaps it was a palace complex for the royal family. Or it could have been a fortress. Nobody knows for sure.

COMPREHENSION

Write your answers on the lines.

1. How did Machu Picchu escape destruction by the Spaniards?

   _____

   _____

2. What mistake was made by the American archeologist Hiram

   Bingham? _____

   _____

3. How were the Incas able to farm the steep mountain slopes?

   _____

4. What was unusual about the huge stones the Incas used in

   their buildings? _____

   _____

5. How did the Incas bring water to their fields? _____

   _____

6. What do the descendents of the Incas have in common with

   their ancestors? _____

   _____

7. What is the main mystery about Machu Picchu that has yet to

   be solved? _____

   _____

VOCABULARY

Circle a letter to show the meaning of each **boldface** word.

1. **inaccessible**

   a. incapable of being reached

   b. unattractive

   c. unfamiliar

   d. inescapable

2. **archeologist**

   a. one who builds arcs

   b. one who draws up plans for cities

   c. one who designs buildings

   d. one who studies the remains of ancient cultures

3. **aqueducts**

   a. shows performed in the water

   b. structures for carrying flowing water

   c. elevated roadways supported on arches

   d. openings in a wall for water to flow through

4. **irrigation**

   a. system for supplying water

   b. method of planting seeds

   c. method of plowing the land

   d. system of protection from rain

5. **plazas**

   a. open-air palaces

   b. covered areas in gardens

   c. open areas near buildings

   d. wide boulevards

6. **shrouded**

   a. shredded   b. sugar-coated   c. shrunken   d. covered

FACT OR OPINION?

Think about the information in the article about Machu Picchu. Read the following statements. Write **F** if the statement is a *fact* or **O** if the statement is an *opinion*.

1. _____ Machu Picchu is truly an amazing sight.

2. _____ Machu Picchu sits at an elevation of 7,710 feet.

3. _____ Perhaps Machu Picchu was a religious ceremonial center.

4. _____ Walkways at Machu Picchu connect the various buildings and terraces.

5. _____ Machu Picchu may have been a palace complex for the royal family.

PUZZLER

Fill in the blanks with words from the article that answer the questions. Then unscramble the circled letters to complete the sentence below the questions. The first one has been done for you.

1. In which mountain range is Machu Picchu located?

  A N D E S

2. Which city was Hiram Bingham searching for?

  __ __ __ __ __ __ __ __ __

3. What is the "old language" of the Incas?

  __ __ __ __ __ __ __

4. Who destroyed the Inca civilization?

  __ __ __ __ __ __ __ __ __

5. Which river is near Machu Picchu?

  __ __ __ __ __ __ __ __

6. What did the Incas cut into the mountain slopes in order to farm there?

  __ __ __ __ __ __ __ __ __

The Incas built stone ___ ___ ___ ___ ___ ___ ___ ___ ___
to bring water to their fields.

DRAWING CONCLUSIONS

Put a checkmark (✔) next to each reasonable conclusion that can be drawn from information in the article.

1. _____ If they had found it, the Spaniards probably would have destroyed Machu Picchu.

2. _____ Machu Picchu could not have been a city, because there were no theaters.

3. _____ The Incas were experts at building with stone.

4. _____ Hiram Bingham was not a very good archeologist.

5. _____ We may never know the original purpose of Machu Picchu.

RECALLING DETAILS

Put a checkmark (✔) in front of the correct answer to each question.

1. What is Machu Picchu's elevation above sea level?

   ____ 2,000 feet

   ____ 7,710 feet

   ____ 10,000 feet

   ____ 20,000 feet

2. How many types of potatoes did the Incas develop?

   ____ 60   ____ 210

   ____ 120   ____ 250

3. What was Hiram Bingham searching for?

   ____ Machu Picchu

   ____ Urubamba

   ____ Vilcabamba

   ____ the Andes

4. What was the language of the Incas known as?

   ____ quipu   ____ Quebec

   ____ Quechua   ____ quiver

━ REVIEW ━

RECALLING SOCIAL STUDIES DETAILS

Circle a letter to show the correct answer to each question.

1. Which of the following California valleys did John Muir plan to explore?

   a. Santa Clara Valley

   b. San Fernando Valley

   c. Yosemite Valley

   d. Great Central Valley

2. The city of Ghent, where the peace treaty ending the War of 1812 was signed, is located in which country?

   a. Great Britain   b. Germany   c. France   d. Belgium

3. Why didn't people in America know that a peace treaty was signed?

   a. Newspaper reporters had not been present at the signing.

   b. There were no telephones or telegraphs in those days.

   c. The negotiators forgot to notify their governments.

   d. The negotiators purposely kept the signing a secret.

4. Which of the following best describes Marco Polo's account of his travels?

   a. Marco Polo actually saw everything he wrote about.

   b. Some of the details were reported to Marco Polo by others.

   c. Marco Polo greatly exaggerated everything he described.

   d. Marco Polo's book had very little to do with the real world.

5. Which of the following items about the lost city of the Incas is true?

   a. Machu Picchu was the real lost city of the Incas.

   b. Vilcabamba was the real lost city of the Incas.

   c. Hiram Bingham believed that Vilcabamba was the lost city.

   d. American archeologists believed Machu Picchu was the lost city.

PREVIEW

HISTORIC SPEECHES

LESSON 1: Patrick Henry: Speech in the Virginia Convention

LESSON 2: Chief Seattle: Speech to the White Man

LESSON 3: Susan B. Anthony: Women's Rights

LESSON 4: Franklin D. Roosevelt: Speech to Congress
(Declaration of War Against Japan)

When you complete this unit, you will be able to answer questions like these:

- *Why did Patrick Henry say he preferred liberty to death?*

- *Why was Chief Seattle willing to live peacefully on a reservation?*

- *Why did Susan B. Anthony say women should vote?*

- *Why did President Roosevelt ask Congress to declare war?*

PRETEST

Write **T** or **F** to show whether you think each statement is *true* or *false*.

1. _____ Patrick Henry said the Americans should not resist British rule.

2. _____ Chief Seattle said his people no longer needed much land because they were now few in number.

3. _____ Chief Seattle believed the red man and the white man should not live apart because they were brothers.

4. _____ Susan B. Anthony was convicted of the "crime" of voting.

5. _____ Susan B. Anthony believed that whether women voted or not, women's rights would be protected by the Constitution.

6. _____ Although the Japanese had attacked the U.S. Navy in Hawaii, Roosevelt believed there was still time to negotiate.

7. _____ President Roosevelt asked Congress to declare war on the Japanese Empire.

Pretest answers: 1.F 2.T 3.F 4.T 5.F 6.F 7.T

PATRICK HENRY: SPEECH TO THE VIRGINIA CONVENTION

Mr. President: No man thinks more highly than I do of the patriotism of the worthy gentlemen who have just addressed the house. But different men often see the same subject in different lights. The question before us is nothing less than a question of freedom or slavery. It is natural to shut our eyes against a painful truth. But is this the part of wise men, engaged in a great struggle for liberty? For my part, I am willing to know the whole truth: to know the worst and to provide for it.

I have but one lamp by which my feet are guided. And that is the lamp of experience. I have no way of judging the future except by the past. Consider the British conduct these last 10 years. What has there been to justify any hopes for the future? Is it that insidious smile with which our petition has been lately received? Trust it not, sir: It will prove a snare to your feet. Suffer not yourselves to be betrayed with a kiss. Is this gracious reception of our petition to be trusted? How does this fit with their warlike preparations that cover our waters and darken our land? Let us not deceive ourselves, sir. Of what purpose are these fleets and armies—if not to force us into submission? Has Great Britain any enemy in this part of the world? No, sir, she has none. Those armies are meant for us.

And what have we to oppose them? Shall we try argument? Sir, we have been trying that for the last 10 years. But it has been all in vain. Sir, we have done everything we could to avert the storm that is now coming on. We have petitioned, but our petitions have been slighted. We have been spurned with contempt from the foot of the throne! In vain may we hope for peace and reconciliation. There is no longer any room for hope.

If we wish to be free, we must fight! I repeat it, sir, we must *fight!* An appeal to God is all that is left us! Some say that we are weak—unable to cope with so formidable an adversary. But when shall we be stronger? Will it be next week, or next year? Will it be when we are totally disarmed? When a British guard shall be stationed in every house? Sir, we are not weak. Three million people are armed in the holy cause of liberty. Surely we are invincible against any force our enemy can send against us. The battle, sir, is not to the strong alone. It is to the vigilant, the active, the brave. Besides, we now have no choice. It is too late to back down. There is no retreat but in submission and slavery! The war is inevitable—and *let it come!* I repeat it, sir, *let it come!*

Why stand we here idle? What is it that gentlemen wish? What would they have? Is life so dear, or peace so sweet, as to be purchased at the price of chains and slavery? Forbid it, Almighty God! I know not what course others may take. But as for me, give me liberty or give me death!

COMPREHENSION

Write **T** if the statement is *true* or **F** if the statement is *false*. Write **NI** for *no information* if the speech does not provide that information.

1. _____ According to Patrick Henry, the members of the Virginia Convention had already agreed to fight Great Britain.

2. _____ According to Patrick Henry, it was better to face the truth rather than to avoid seeing it.

3. _____ Patrick Henry advised the delegates not to be deceived by the British response to their recent petition.

4. _____ Patrick Henry wondered how the British could remain friendly while the Americans made preparations for war.

5. _____ For many years, Patrick Henry had been urging Americans to fight for independence from Britain.

6. _____ Patrick Henry became a lawyer after his farm had been destroyed by fire.

7. _____ According to Patrick Henry, the Americans had done everything possible to avoid war with Britain.

8. _____ Patrick Henry believed it was still possible to reach a compromise with Great Britain.

9. _____ Patrick Henry believed it was too late to avoid war with Britain.

10. _____ Patrick Henry felt that death was preferable to life under British rule.

DRAWING CONCLUSIONS

Put a checkmark (✔) next to each reasonable conclusion that can be drawn from information in the speech.

1. _____ Patrick Henry was willing to give up his life in a fight for freedom from Great Britain.

2. _____ In order to keep the peace, the British were willing to give in to America's demands.

3. _____ Patrick Henry believed the Americans would be outnumbered by the British, and had little chance of winning a war.

4. _____ It was worth paying any price in order for Americans to keep the peace and stay alive.

RECOGNIZING PERSUASIVE DEVICES

Asking questions is one effective method of persuasion. This forces the listener to think about what the speaker is saying. Find the following questions in Patrick Henry's speech. Then, on the lines below, write Patrick Henry's answers to his own questions.

1. *Of what purpose are these fleets and armies, if not to force us into submission? Has Great Britain any enemy in this part of the world?*

   _____

2. *And what have we to oppose them? Shall we try argument?*

   _____

3. *But when shall we be stronger? Will it be next week, or next year? Will it be when we are totally disarmed? When a British guard shall be stationed in every house?* _____

   _____

   _____

4. *Is life so dear, or peace so sweet, as to be purchased at the price of chains and slavery?* _____

   _____

   _____

VOCABULARY

Read the **boldface** words on the left. Then write a letter to match each word with its definition on the right. The first one has been done for you.

1. _j_ **patriotism**   a. opponent, enemy

2. _____ **reconciliation**   b. giving in to the control of another

3. _____ **contempt**   c. treacherous

4. _____ **adversary**   d. mighty

5. _____ **vigilant**   e. undefeatable

6. _____ **inevitable**   f. renewal of friendship

7. _____ **snare**   g. rejected with contempt

8. _____ **petition**   h. compassionate

9. _____ **invincible**   i. scorn, disdain

10. _____ **insidious**   j. love for one's country

11. _____ **formidable**   k. written request

12. _____ **spurned**   l. watchful

13. _____ **deceive**   m. trap

14. _____ **submission**   n. unavoidable

15. _____ **gracious**   o. mislead

PUZZLER

Two or more words in each sentence are written backward. Find these words, circle them, and write them correctly on the lines below. The first one is done for you.

1. It is (larutan) to shut our eyes against a (lufniap) truth.

   natural   _painful_

2. Is it that suoidisni smile with which our noititep has been received?

_____

3. Suffer not sevlesruoy to be deyarteb with a kiss.

_____

4. We have been denrups with tpmetnoc from the foot of the enorht!

_____

5. There is no taerter but in noissimbus and yrevals!

_____

RECALLING DETAILS

Circle a letter to correctly answer each question.

1. Patrick Henry's feet were guided by which lamp?

   a. the lamp near the door   c. the lamp in the kitchen

   b. the lamp of experience   d. the lamp in the bedroom

2. According to Patrick Henry, what would the Americans have
   to do if they wished to be free?

   a. negotiate with the British   c. fight the British

   b. send another petition   d. move farther west and
      to Britain   build new colonies

3. According to Patrick Henry, how many Americans were
   available to fight the British?

   a. 3,000   b. 30,000   c. 300,000   d. 3,000,000

Before reading . . .

Seattle was a great chief of the Duwamish and Suquamish tribes of the Pacific Northwest. On January 12, 1854, he spoke about the changes facing his people and called out for justice. Read the adapted excerpt from his speech. Notice that Seattle uses *similes* to make direct comparisons between two subjects.

Death Mask of
Chief Seattle

CHIEF SEATTLE:
SPEECH TO THE WHITE MAN

Yonder sky, which has wept tears of compassion on our fathers for centuries untold, and which to us looks eternal, may change. Today it is fair; tomorrow it may be overcast with clouds. My words are like the stars that never set. What Seattle says, the great chief in Washington can rely upon with as much certainty as the return of the seasons. The son of the white chief says his father sends us greetings of friendship and good will. This is kind, for his people are many. We know he has little need of our friendship in return. The white man is like the grass that covers the vast prairies. My people, however, are few, like the scattering trees of a windswept plain.

The great white chief sends word that he wants to buy our lands. And he is willing to allow us to reserve enough to live on comfortably. This appears generous—for the red man no longer has rights that he need respect. The offer may also be wise—for we are no longer in need of a great country. Once our people covered the whole land as the waves of a wind-ruffled sea cover its shell floor. But that time has long since passed away. The greatness of our tribes is almost forgotten. I will not reproach my paleface brothers for this, for we may have been somewhat to blame.

When our young men grow angry and go on the warpath, their cruelty knows no bounds. Our old men are unable to restrain them. But let us hope that hostilities between the red man and his paleface brothers may never return. We would have everything to lose and nothing to gain. Our young braves believe that revenge is a worthy goal. But old men who stay at home in times of war—and old women who have sons to lose—know better.

If we do as he wishes, the great chief in Washington promises to protect us. He says he will be our father and we will be his children. But can this ever be? Your God loves your people and hates mine. He makes your people stronger every day. Soon they will fill the land. But the white man's God cannot love his red children, or he would protect them. How, then, can we become brothers? Your God came to the white man. We never saw him; never even heard his voice. He gave the white man laws, but he had no word for his red children. No, we are two distinct races and must ever remain so. There is little in common between us. Day and night cannot dwell together. The red man has ever fled the approach of the white man—as the changing mists on the mountainside flee before the blazing morning sun.

Your proposal, however, seems a just one. I think my people will accept it. We will retire to the reservation you offer us. We will dwell apart and in peace. It matters little where we pass the remainder of our days. No bright star hovers about the horizon. Sad-voiced winds moan in the distance. Men come and go like waves of the sea. Even the white man is not exempt from this common destiny. We may be brothers after all. We shall see.

COMPREHENSION

Write your answers in complete sentences.

1. What message did Chief Seattle receive from the great white chief in Washington? _____

   _____

2. Why did Chief Seattle say the offer from Washington was *generous?* _____

   _____

3. Why did Chief Seattle say the offer from Washington might also have been *wise?* _____

   _____

4. Why did Chief Seattle hope that hostilities between red men and white men would never return? _____

   _____

5. Why did Chief Seattle believe the red man and the white man had little in common? _____

   _____

6. How did Chief Seattle believe his people would respond to the white man's offer? _____

   _____

7. What did Chief Seattle mean when he said, "Men come and go like the waves of the sea"? _____

   _____

IDENTIFYING SIMILES

A *simile* is a figure of speech that uses *like* or *as* to make a direct comparison between two subjects. Read the first parts of several similes Chief Seattle used. Then find the similes in the speech. Finally, write down the second part of each simile.

1. My words are like _____.

2. His people are many. They are like _____

_____.

3. My people are few, like _____

_____.

4. Once our people covered the whole land as _____

_____.

5. The red man has ever fled the approach of the white man, as

_____

_____.

6. Men come and go like _____.

IDENTIFYING PARTS OF SPEECH

Nouns are words that name a person, place, or thing. *Verbs* are words that describe an action or state of being. Read the **boldface** words. Write **N** if the word is a *noun* or **V** if the word is a *verb*.

____ **fathers**	____ **centuries**	____ **wept**	____ **people**
____ **covers**	____ **sends**	____ **friendship**	____ **appears**
____ **passed**	____ **warpath**	____ **protect**	____ **children**
____ **retire**	____ **brothers**	____ **horizon**	____ **remain**

DRAWING CONCLUSIONS

Put a checkmark (✔) next to each reasonable conclusion that can be drawn from information in the speech.

1. _____ Chief Seattle planned to trick the white chief in Washington by pretending to accept his offer.

2. _____ Chief Seattle believed revenge was not a worthy goal.

3. _____ Chief Seattle believed his people could count on the white man's God for protection.

4. _____ Chief Seattle believed the red man and the white man were better off living apart.

SENTENCE COMPLETION

Choose 10 words from the box to complete the sentences below.

compassion	destiny	generous	hostilities
restrain	revenge	distinct	reservation
remainder	blazing	horizon	comfortably

1. We will retire to the _____ you offer us.

2. Yonder sky has wept tears of _____ on our fathers.

3. Our young braves believe that _____ is a worthy goal.

4. Even the white man is not exempt from this common _____.

5. This offer appears to be _____.

6. He will reserve land we can live on _____.

94

7. It matters little where we pass the _____ of our days.

8. We are two _____ races and must ever remain so.

9. Let us hope that _____ may never return.

10. No bright star hovers about the _____.

PUZZLER

Fill in the blanks with words from the speech. Then unscramble the circled letters to learn the name of the "great white chief in Washington." The answer will name the U.S. president who was in office at the time of Chief Seattle's speech. The first one has been done for you.

1. Chief Seattle said that day and night cannot D W $\boxed{E}$ L L together.

2. The son of the great white chief says his father sends greetings of

   __ __ __ __ __ __ __ __ __ .

3. According to Chief Seattle, the great white chief's offer may

   also be __ __ __ __ .

4. When young men go on the warpath, their

   __ __ __ __ __ __ __ knows no bounds.

5. According to Chief Seattle, the white men are like the grass that

   covers the vast __ __ __ __ __ __ __ .

The name of the "great white chief" in Washington:

__ __ __ __ __ __

Before reading . . .

Susan B. Anthony was a long-time champion of women's rights. In 1872, she led a group of women to the polls to vote in the presidential election. At the time, women in the United States had not yet won the right to vote. Anthony was indicted and convicted of the "crime" of voting. As you read this adapted excerpt from her speech, notice how she defended her actions by asserting her equal rights as a citizen.

SUSAN B. ANTHONY: WOMEN'S RIGHTS

Friends and fellow citizens, I stand before you tonight under indictment. My crime is having voted at the last presidential election. It is said that I do not have a lawful right to vote. It shall be my work this evening to prove to you that I committed no crime. Instead, I simply exercised my citizen's rights. These rights are guaranteed to me and to all U.S. citizens by the Constitution—beyond the power of any state to deny.

The preamble of the federal Constitution says:

"We, the people of the United States, in order to form a more perfect union, establish justice, insure domestic tranquillity, provide for the common defense, promote the general welfare, and secure the blessings of liberty to ourselves and our posterity, do ordain and establish this Constitution for the United States of America."

It was we, the people—not we, the white male citizens; nor yet we, the male citizens—but we, *the whole people*, who formed the Union. And we formed it, not to give the blessings of liberty, but to secure them. Liberty was not granted to half of ourselves and half of our posterity, but to *the whole people*—women as well as men. Yet women are denied the only means of securing their rights provided by this democratic-republican government—the ballot. It is downright mockery to talk of women enjoying the blessings of liberty under such a circumstance.

For any state to make sex a qualification is a violation of the supreme law of the land. Such states forever withhold the blessings of liberty from women and their female posterity. To these states, this government is not a democracy. It is not a republic. It is an odious aristocracy— a hateful oligarchy of sex. I say it is the most hateful aristocracy ever established on the face of the globe. It is an oligarchy of wealth, where the rich govern the poor. It is an oligarchy of sex that makes father, brothers, husband, and sons the oligarchs over the mother and sisters, the wife and daughters of every household. It ordains all men sovereigns and all women subjects. It carries dissension, discord, and rebellion into every home of the nation.

The dictionary defines a citizen as a person in the United States who is entitled to vote and hold office. The only question left to be settled now is this: *Are women persons?* I can hardly believe any of our opponents will have the hardihood to say they are not. Being persons, then, women *are* citizens. And no state has a right to make any law, or to enforce any old law, that shall abridge their privileges or immunities. Hence, every discrimination against women in the constitutions and laws of the individual states is today null and void—precisely as is every law against Negroes.

COMPREHENSION

Write your answers in complete sentences.

1. What crime was Susan B. Anthony accused of? _____

    _____

2. Why does Susan B. Anthony believe she has not committed a crime?

    _____

    _____

3. According to Susan B. Anthony, which people formed the Union?

    _____

    _____

4. According to Susan B. Anthony, why was the Union formed in the

    first place? _____

    _____

5. Why did Susan B. Anthony believe it was a mockery to say that

    women enjoyed the blessings of liberty? _____

    _____

6. According to Susan B. Anthony, a state that makes sex a

    qualification for voting is violating what law? _____

    _____

7. Why did Susan B. Anthony describe as "hateful" a government

    based on an oligarchy of sex? _____

    _____

    _____

VOCABULARY

Circle a letter to show the meaning of each **boldface** word.

1. **tranquillity**
   a. calmness, stability
   b. tension
   c. reliability
   d. turbulence

2. **secure**
   a. separate
   b. sure of
   c. to guarantee
   d. to withhold

3. **posterity**
   a. possessions
   b. all future generations
   c. progress
   d. inheritance

4. **odious**
   a. odorous
   b. open-ended
   c. odd
   d. hateful

5. **oligarchy**
   a. rule by a few
   b. rule by several political parties
   c. dictatorship
   d. rule by majority vote

6. **sovereigns**
   a. socialists
   b. supreme rulers
   c. Southerners
   d. sports fans

7. **hardihood**
   a. nerve, audacity
   b. generosity
   c. thoughtfulness
   d. spitefulness

8. **abridge**
   a. build upon
   b. connect
   c. diminish, reduce
   d. nullify

DRAWING CONCLUSIONS

Put a checkmark (✔) next to each reasonable conclusion that could be drawn from information in the speech.

1. _____ Like all guilty people, Susan B. Anthony tried to convince others of her innocence.

2. _____ Susan B. Anthony was a great believer in the ideas and ideals of the U.S. Constitution.

3. _____ According to Susan B. Anthony, being able to vote was the only way that women in America could enjoy the blessings of liberty.

4. _____ Susan B. Anthony wanted American women to have equal rights to become oligarches.

5. _____ According to Susan B. Anthony, men's absolute power over women could only lead to trouble in the home.

6. _____ The dictionary gives U.S. citizens the right to vote and to hold office.

7. _____ Since women are persons, they must be given the rights granted to all citizens, including the right to vote.

FORMING PLURAL ENDINGS

Add -s or -ies to write the plural form (names more than one) next to each **boldface** word.

1. **citizen** _____
2. **dictionary** _____
3. **husband** _____
4. **aristocracy** _____
5. **person** _____

6. **oligarchy** _____
7. **republic** _____
8. **violation** _____
9. **blessing** _____
10. **household** _____

ANTONYMS

Antonyms are words that have opposite meanings. In each group of words, circle the antonym of the **boldface** word.

1. **question**   query   inquiry   answer   problem

2. **sovereigns**   kings   rulers   emperors   subjects

3. **established**   founded   ended   begun   built

4. **withhold**   give   withdraw   withstand   hide

5. **denied**   deprived   allowed   destroyed   dropped

6. **wealth**   riches   money   treasure   poverty

PUZZLER

Use the clues to help you complete the crossword puzzle. Answers are words
that complete the sentences.

ACROSS

1. The Union was formed
   by the _____ people,
   women as well as men.

5. _____ against women is
   unconstitutional.

7. Susan B. Anthony was
   _____ for committing a
   crime.

DOWN

2. By voting, Susan B. Anthony
   _____ her citizen's rights.

3. The right to vote is _____ by
   the Constitution.

4. Since women are persons,
   they are also _____.

6. A government that withholds
   from women the right to vote
   is an _____ of sex.

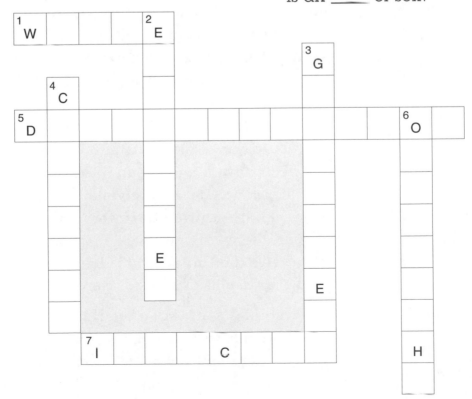

Before reading . . .

On December 8, 1941, President Franklin D. Roosevelt delivered a famous speech. He spoke to the U.S. Congress in response to Japan's surprise attack against U.S. forces on the island of Oahu in Hawaii. As you read this adapted excerpt, notice how Roosevelt builds a persuasive argument for declaring war on Japan.

FRANKLIN D. ROOSEVELT: SPEECH TO CONGRESS
(Declaration of War Against Japan)

Mr. Vice-President, Mr. Speaker, members of the Senate and the House of Representatives: Yesterday, December 7, 1941—a date which will live in infamy—the United States of America was suddenly and deliberately attacked by naval and air forces of the empire of Japan. We were then in conversation with the Japanese government regarding the maintenance of peace in the Pacific.

Just one hour after Japanese air squadrons had commenced bombing the American island of Oahu, the Japanese ambassador to the United States delivered to our secretary of state a formal reply to a recent American message. This reply stated that it seemed useless to continue the existing negotiations. But it contained no threat or hint of war or armed attack. The distance between Hawaii and Japan makes it obvious that the attack was deliberately planned many days or weeks ago. During the intervening time, the Japanese government has deliberately sought to deceive the United States by false statements and expressions of hope for continued peace.

Yesterday's attack on the Hawaiian Islands has caused severe damage to American naval and military forces. I regret to tell you that very many American lives have been lost. In addition,

American ships have been reported torpedoed. Those attacks were made on the high seas between San Francisco and Honolulu.

Yesterday, the Japanese also launched an attack against Malaya. Last night, Japanese forces attacked Hong Kong, Guam, the Philippine Islands, and Wake Island. And this morning the Japanese have attacked Midway Island. Japan has therefore undertaken a surprise offensive throughout the Pacific area. The facts of yesterday and today speak for themselves. The people of the United States have already formed their opinions. They well understand the implications to the very life and safety of our nation.

As commander and chief of the army and navy, I have directed that all measures be taken for our defense. Always will our nation remember the character of the onslaught against us. No matter how long it may take, we are resolved to overcome this premeditated invasion. In their righteous might, the American people will win through to absolute victory. I believe that I interpret the will of the Congress and of the people when I assert that we will not only defend ourselves to the uttermost. We will also make it very certain that this form of treachery shall never again endanger us.

Hostilities exist. There is no blinking at the fact that our people, our territory, and our interests are in grave danger. Yet we have confidence in our armed forces, and the unbounding determination of our people. We *will* gain the inevitable triumph, so help us God. I ask that the Congress declare that since the unprovoked and dastardly attack by Japan on Sunday, December 7, 1941, a state of war has existed between the United States and the Japanese Empire.

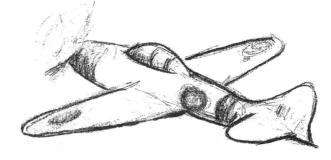

COMPREHENSION

Write **T** if the statement is *true* or **F** if the statement is *false*. Write **NI** for *no information* if the speech does not provide that information.

1. _____ The United States had plenty of warning that the Japanese were planning to attack Hawaii.

2. _____ The United States had been attempting to maintain peaceful relations with Japan.

3. _____ The Japanese military leader who planned the attack on Hawaii was Admiral Isoroku Yamamoto.

4. _____ The Japanese had planned the attack while at the same time pretending to be interested in peace.

5. _____ Some 2,400 Americans were killed and more than 1,000 were wounded in the Japanese attack.

6. _____ President Roosevelt was certain that Congress and the American people would support a declaration of war against Japan.

SENTENCE COMPLETION

Choose nine words from the box to complete the sentences below.

premeditated	torpedoed	infamy	commenced
onslaught	dastardly	offensive	deliberately
solicitation	inevitable	implications	righteous

1. Americans well understand the _____ to the

   life and safety of the nation.

2. The Japanese government has _____ sought

   to deceive the United States.

3. Japanese air squadrons _____ bombing the American island of Oahu.

4. The American people, in their _____ might, will win through to absolute victory.

5. Japan has undertaken a surprise _____ throughout the Pacific area.

6. With the unbounding determination of our people, we will gain the _____ triumph.

7. American ships have been reported _____ on the high seas.

8. Always will our nation remember the character of the _____ against us.

9. According to President Roosevelt, December 7, 1941, is a date that will live in _____.

DRAWING CONCLUSIONS

Put a checkmark (✔) next to each reasonable conclusion that can be drawn from the information in the speech.

1. _____ The Japanese attacked because they felt there was more to be gained through war than through peaceful relations.

2. _____ The American military forces in Hawaii were not prepared for the Japanese attack.

3. _____ The Japanese attack provoked anger and outrage among the American people.

4. _____ The fact that the Japanese attacked so many places suggested that they were planning to create a huge empire.

5. _____ The Americans knew what the Japanese were up to and only pretended to take the peace negotiations seriously.

RECALLING DETAILS

Circle a letter to show the correct answer to each question.

1. Which of the following Hawaiian islands did the Japanese begin bombing?

   a. Maui   b. Molokai   c. Oahu   d. Kauai

2. Which of the following places was **not** attacked by the Japanese?

   a. Guam   b. Tahiti   c. Hong Kong   d. Malaya

3. American ships were reported to have been torpedoed while sailing between which two cities?

   a. San Francisco and Los Angeles

   b. Honolulu and Los Angeles

   c. San Francisco and Honolulu

   d. Honolulu and Seattle

4. To whom did the Japanese ambassador deliver a formal reply to a recent American message?

   a. the president

   b. the secretary of state

   c. the secretary of defense

   d. the attorney general

PUZZLER

Fill in the blanks with words from the speech. Then unscramble the circled letters to learn the name of the primary target of the Japanese attack on Hawaii. The first one has been done for you.

1. The Japanese reply contained no __T__ __H__ __R__ __E__ __A__ __T__ of war.

2. The Japanese government __ __ __ __ __ __ __ __ __ __ __ __ sought to deceive the United States.

3. The __ __ __ __ __ __ on Hawaii caused severe damage.

4. American ships were reported __ __ __ __ __ __ __ __ __ on the high seas.

5. The United States was attacked by Japanese naval and air __ __ __ __ __ __.

6. The attack was __ __ __ __ __ __ __ weeks before it took place.

7. Many Americans were killed during the __ __ __ __ __ __ __ __ of Oahu.

8. The Japanese ambassador __ __ __ __ __ __ __ __ __ a formal reply.

9. President Roosevelt believed that he had correctly __ __ __ __ __ __ __ __ __ __ __ the will of the Congress and the American people.

The primary target of the Japanese attack on Hawaii:

__ __ __ __ __ __ __   __ __ __ __ __ __

107

REVIEW

RECALLING DETAILS ABOUT HISTORIC SPEECHES

Circle a letter to show the correct answer to each question.

1. Which one of the following would Patrick Henry have chosen?

   a. peace at the price of chains and slavery

   b. life at any price

   c. death rather than the chains of slavery

   d. submission to British rule

2. What persuasive device did Patrick Henry use throughout his speech?

   a. similes

   b. metaphors

   c. questions to make his listeners think

   d. reliance on statistics to prove his points

3. What literary device did Chief Seattle use throughout his speech?

   a. metaphors

   b. similes

   c. personifications

   d. questions and answers

4. Which historic document did Susan B. Anthony quote in her speech?

   a. the Declaration of Independence

   b. the preamble of the Constitution

   c. the Bill of Rights

   d. the Declaration of the Rights of Man

5. Which words did President Roosevelt use in his speech to describe the Japanese surprise attack on Oahu in Hawaii?

   a. cowardly, deliberate, calculated, provocative

   b. deliberate, premeditated, dastardly, unprovoked

   c. calculated, deliberate, outrageous, destructive

   d. deliberate, provocative, dastardly, cowardly

GLOSSARY OF READING TERMS

adapted rewritten to be made shorter or easier to read

alliteration repetition of the initial sound in two or more words; a poetic device

analyze to identify and examine the separate parts of a whole

author's purpose the writer's specific goal or reason for writing a particular book, article, etc.

categorize to divide into main subjects or groups

cause a happening or situation that makes something else happen as a result

classify to organize according to some similarity

compare to make note of how two or more things are alike

compound word a word made by combining two or more smaller words

conclusion the end or last part of a novel, article, etc.

context clues the words in a sentence just before and after an unfamiliar word or phrase. Context clues help to make clear what the unfamiliar word means.

contrast to make note of how two or more things are different from one another

describe to tell or write about something or someone in detail in order to help the reader or listener create a mental image

details bits of information or description that support the main idea and make it clearer

dialogue lines spoken by characters in a story or play

discuss to talk or write about a topic, giving various opinions and ideas

effect the reaction or impact that occurs as a result of a cause

elements the essential parts or components of a whole

excerpt section quoted from a book, article, etc.

fact something that actually happened or is really true

fiction literary work in which the plot and characters are imagined by the author

figurative language colorful, nonliteral use of words and phrases to achieve a dramatic effect

generalize to form a general rule or idea after considering particular facts

graphs charts or diagrams that visually present changes in something or the relationship between two or more changing things

homonyms words pronounced alike but having different meanings and usually different spellings

identify to name or point out; to distinguish someone or something from others

image idea, impression; a picture in the mind

inference conclusion arrived at by careful reasoning

interpret to explain the meaning of; to figure out in one's own way

judgment a decision made after weighing various facts

literature the entire body of written work including fiction, nonfiction, drama, poetry, etc.

locate find; tell where something is

main idea the point or central thought in a written work or part of a work

multiple-meaning words lookalike words that have different meanings in different contexts

nonfiction writing about the real world, real people, actual events, etc.

objective reflecting what is actual or real; expressed without bias or opinion

order items arranged or sequenced in a certain way, such as alphabetical order or order of importance

organize to put in place according to a system

outcome the result; the way that something turns out

parts of speech grammatical classifications of eight word types: adjective, adverb, conjunction, interjection, noun, preposition, pronoun, or verb

passage section of a written work

plot the chain of events in a story that leads to the story's outcome

plural word form showing more than one person, place, or thing

point of view the position from which something is observed or told; when a character tells the story, *first person* point of view is used; an author who tells the story in his own voice is using *third person* point of view.

predict to foretell what you think will happen in the future

prefix group of letters added at the beginning of a word to change the word's meaning or function

recall to remember or bring back to mind

refer to speak of something or call attention to it

relationship a connection of some kind between two or more persons, things, events, etc.

scan to glance at something or look over it quickly

sequence items in order; succession; one thing following another

singular word form naming just one person, place, or thing

subjective reflecting personal ideas, opinions, or experiences

suffix group of letters added at the end of a word that changes the word's meaning or function

symbol a concrete object used to represent an abstract idea

table an orderly, graphic arrangement of facts, figures, etc.

tense verb form that shows the time of the action, such as past, present, or future

term word or phrase with a special meaning in a certain field of study such as art, history, etc.

tone the feeling given by the author's choice of language

vocabulary all the words of a language